Implementation Science

The Improvement Science in Education Series

Improvement Science (IS) originated in such fields as engineering and health care, but its principal foundation has been found to be an effective school improvement methodology in education. Although improvement science research is quickly becoming a signature pedagogy and core subject area of inquiry in the field of educational leadership, the literature is still scant in its coverage of IS models. The Improvement Science in Education series is intended to be the most comprehensive collection of volumes to inform educators and researchers about problem analysis, utilization of research, development of solutions, and other practices that can be employed to enhance and strengthen efforts at organizational improvement. This series concentrates on the elements faculty, students, and administrators need to enhance the reliability and validity of improvement or quality enhancement efforts.

Books in the Series

The Educational Leader's Guide to Improvement Science: Data, Design, and Cases for Reflection
by Robert Crow, Brandi Nicole Hinnant-Crawford, and Dean T. Spaulding (2019)

The Improvement Science Dissertation in Practice: A Guide for Faculty, Committee Members, and their Students
by Jill Alexa Perry, Debby Zambo, and Robert Crow (2020)

Improvement Science in Education: A Primer
by Brandi Nicole Hinnant-Crawford (2020)

Teaching Improvement Science in Educational Leadership: A Pedagogical Guide
by Dean T. Spaulding, Robert Crow, and Brandi Nicole Hinnant-Crawford (2021)

Improvement Science: Promoting Equity in Schools
by Deborah S. Peterson and Susan P. Carlile (2021)

Improvement Science as a Tool for School Enhancement: Solutions for Better Educational Outcomes
by Deborah S. Peterson and Susan P. Carlile (2025)

Improvement Science in Education: A Primer - 2nd Edition
by Brandi Hinnant-Crawford (2025)

Advancing Special Education Through Improvement Science: A Practical Guide
by Antonio L. Ellis and Sarah Irvine Belson (2025)

Implementation Science: A Playbook for Instructional Leaders
by Julia Carlson (2025)

The Teaching and Learning of Collaborative Continuous Improvement in Education
by Kristen Campbell Wilcox, Elizabeth Zumpe, and David H. Eddy-Spicer (2026)

Editorial submissions

Authors interested in having their manuscripts considered for publication in the Improvement Science in Education Series are encouraged to send a prospectus, sample chapter, and CV to any one of the series editors:
Robert Crow (rcrow@email.wcu.edu),
Brandi Nicole Hinnant-Crawford (bnhinnantcrawford@email.wcu.edu),
or Dean T. Spaulding (ds6494@yahoo.com).

ADVANCE PRAISE FOR

Implementation Science:
A Playbook for Instructional Leaders

"Drawing upon her rich experiences as a school leader, Dr. Julia Carlson deftly translates the big ideas of implementation science into a clear, thought-provoking guide. Reflection questions and real-world examples woven into each chapter book invite readers into walking the walk of data-informed improvement. This playbook offers an excellent starting point for leaders ready to make meaningful, lasting change in their schools."

Vincent Cho, Ph.D.,
Boston College

"Dr. Julia Carlson brings remarkable authenticity and clarity to the world of implementation science. This book weaves historical context, research, and her rich leadership experiences, in a way that is both deeply personal and highly practical. This isn't a book you read once and shelve—it's a playbook leaders will return to again and again for professional development, strategic planning, and instructional support. With digestible insights and implementable strategies, it's poised to transform not only how schools function, but how students thrive."

Alison Divino Driscoll,
Curriculum and Instruction Manager specializing
in learning design and instructional leadership

"In *Implementation Science: A Playbook for Instructional Leaders*, Dr. Julia Carlson masterfully blends the rigor of research with the realities of school leadership. Grounded in the principles of implementation science, this book is a trusted companion for leaders committed to meaningful, measurable change. Through compelling case studies, actionable strategies, and thoughtful reflection questions, Dr. Carlson empowers school and district leaders to move from ideas to impact. This playbook is essential for anyone engaged in the challenging work of school improvement. Dr. Carlson doesn't just point to the "what"; she illuminates the "how" in a way that's both practical and powerful."

Lori McEwen, Ph.D.,
University of Massachusetts Dartmouth

Implementation Science

A Playbook for Instructional Leaders

BY Julia Carlson

Myers Education Press

Gorham, Maine

Myers Education Press

Published by Myers Education Press, LLC
P.O. Box 424
Gorham, ME 04038

Myers Education Press is an academic publisher specializing in books, e-books, and digital content in the field of education. All of our books are subjected to a rigorous peer review process and produced in compliance with the standards of the Council on Library and Information Resources.

Library of Congress Cataloging-in-Publication Data available from Library of Congress.

13-digit ISBN 978-1-9755-0806-7 (paperback)
13-digit ISBN 978-1-9755-0807-4 (library networkable e-edition)
13-digit ISBN 978-1-9755-0808-1 (consumer e-edition)

Printed in the United States of America.

All first editions printed on acid-free paper that meets the American National Standards Institute Z39-48 standard.

Books published by Myers Education Press may be purchased at special quantity discount rates for groups, workshops, training organizations, and classroom usage. Please call our customer service department at 1-800-232-0223 for details.

Cover design by Green Frog Publishing.

Visit us on the web at **www.myersedpress.com** to browse our complete list of titles.

DEDICATION

To the scores of educators, leaders, and changemakers I have had the privilege of serving and standing by, who strive to make meaningful, lasting impacts on the lives of students and communities, your commitment to learning and growth inspires the future.

To Jacques and Julian, who always believed in their mom.

And to those who dare to bridge the gap between vision and action—may this book serve as a guide and a reminder that every step forward counts.

CONTENTS

LIST OF FIGURES

ACKNOWLEDGMENTS

Writing *Implementation Science: A Playbook for Instructional Leaders* has been an incredible journey, one that would not have been possible without the lived experiences, support, guidance, and encouragement of many remarkable individuals. I am deeply grateful to everyone who has contributed to making this book a reality. I would like to take this opportunity to acknowledge and thank those who have been instrumental along the way.

First and foremost, I owe my family an outstanding debt of gratitude—my husband and two wonderful sons. To my husband, thank you for your sacrifices to raise strong young men who seek to explore and understand this world. You have offered me endless encouragement, patience, and understanding. You have been my rock throughout our incredible 25 years together, offering your love and support every step of the way. To my sons Jacques and Julian, thank you for filling my life with joy, curiosity, and inspiration. Watching you grow and learn has been a constant reminder of why I am so passionate about the future of education. You are my greatest motivation, and I dedicate this work in part to you, hoping it contributes to a brighter, more equitable educational landscape. Finally, I entered the education field because of my amazing sister, JJ Holman. I remember visiting her classroom as a guest speaker and seeing firsthand the impact one great teacher can make. She changed the course of my life.

I am a practitioner at heart, so I would be remiss not to express my heartfelt gratitude to my former colleagues who pushed me and brought clarity to often dark times. Siobhan Dennis, you are like a breath of fresh air. What fun we had traveling and presenting what we truly believed in and knew could have positive impacts. Your insights, passion for education, and commitment to excellence have shaped the foundation of my work. Dean Cevallos, my first mentor principal at Kea'au High School on the Big Island of Hawaii, gave me the autonomy to innovate with ongoing guidance and support. In addition, you taught me all about academic and financial plans and the importance of understanding the *through* line from the district, site, and classroom. You made me curious and relentless in supporting students. To Betsy Furtado, K.C. Perry, Jon Mendelsohn, Cristina Yates, and Ann Marie Deady, you will always hold a special place in my heart. "Once a Knight, Always a Knight." Our time at Central was some of the toughest, funniest, craziest, and most instructional experiences I have had. Paula Soares, you made me smile through tough times and focus on what we could change, not what we couldn't. I truly know that every situation is a lesson to learn from. To Jennifer Gonzales and Corinne Neil, you saw the importance and value of an emerging field and jumped in with both feet. To the rock stars Alison Driscoll, Allison Escher, Sonia Lombre-Odom, Lizzie Brady, Taylor Willet, Lauren Keeling, Heidi Jo McManaman, and Sara Norman, I hope our paths cross again. To these ladies and gentlemen, the collaborative spirit, thoughtful discussions, and shared vision we developed while working together have profoundly influenced my understanding of educational leadership and the importance of Implementation Science. I have been privileged to learn from each of you, and your dedication to improving student outcomes continues to inspire me. Thank you for challenging me to think critically, pushing me to grow, and supporting me throughout this journey.

In addition to my colleagues and family, I would like to acknowledge the many educators, administrators, and instructional leaders who have dedicated themselves to improving schools and districts. This work is *not* easy. Your commitment to transformative change, openness to new ideas, and resilience in the face of challenges have all influenced the direction of this book. I am particularly grateful to those who have shared their experiences, insights, and feedback with me. Through your stories and efforts, I have been able to understand better the practical applications of Implementation Science in real-world educational settings.

Finally, to all the readers of this playbook, thank you for your dedication to improving education for all students. I hope this book is valuable as you continue your journey toward meaningful, sustainable change in your schools and districts. Your work is vital, and I sincerely hope that the strategies, tools, and insights shared in these pages will empower you to lead with confidence and vision.

To everyone who has been part of this journey—thank you. Your support, wisdom, and belief in the importance of this work have made *Implementation Science: A Playbook for Instructional Leaders* a reality, and I am forever grateful.

FOREWORD

As a former school principal, I have spent great energy, with varying success, over the years leading schools through new curriculum adoptions and the implementation of interventions. At that time, I was unaware that there was a formula of success that could be used as a framework to help support these efforts. It was only later in my career as a school administrator that I learned about Implementation Science and its impact to bring a systematic approach to drive instructional change for school improvement at scale.

Implementation Science is the study of methods and strategies to promote the adoption and integration of evidence-based practices in real-world settings. The goal of Implementation Science in education is to provide all students access to high-quality and effective instruction. It provides a framework that serves as the critical bridge between research and practice to ensure that the benefits of evidence-based curricula or innovations can be fully realized and effectively translated. In today's world, increasingly driven by data and student proficiency, the ability to implement evidence-based solutions holds profound significance. In its simplest terms, a student cannot benefit from an intervention they do not receive. Integrity of implementation is the key for students to experience the expected benefits of an intervention, and Implementation Science is the driver to provide the structure to help make it happen.

Implementation Science: A Playbook for Instructional Leaders, written by my colleague and friend, Dr. Julia Carlson, a researcher and practitioner who knows the challenges of leading schools, describes a step-by-step methodology for school and district leaders who are looking for a systematic approach to leading significant instructional change. Julia and I have had the opportunity to collaborate and work with talented and committed educators across the country to bring awareness of Implementation Science, focusing on early literacy development as a lever for school improvement.

Implementation Science is a dynamic and evolving discipline, with vast potential to shape the future of evidence-based practice. As new challenges emerge, so too will the need for innovative strategies and collaborative efforts. This playbook provides readers with the step-by-step foundation to plan, select, implement, monitor, and assess interventions with integrity, ensuring they help as many students as possible realize the full potential of the intervention.

I invite my fellow school and district leaders to examine the status of the practices within your setting that contribute to a healthy implementation of the curriculum or intervention. Do you have an effective evidence-based practice, effective implementation of that practice, and the enabling context within the system to support and fully realize the intended outcomes? All three comprise the formula for elevating student outcomes, and *Implementation Science: A Playbook for Instructional Leaders* will guide you through the process to achieve that success.

Dr. Carlson's text is an invitation for all school leaders to contribute to this ongoing journey, fostering a community of practice that prioritizes learning, adaptation, and impact. Together, we can ensure that the promise of research translates into meaningful, sustainable change where effective practice and implementation aligned with a shared responsibility of enabling context allows all students to succeed.

—Dr. Siobhan M. Dennis

PREFACE

Implementation Science: A Playbook for Instructional Leaders

Throughout my career, I have approached challenges and opportunities with a mindset shaped by what some might call an "upside-down and backward" view of the world. This phrase, born from my earliest struggles with literacy, encapsulates a way of seeing problems not as insurmountable but as puzzles to be reimagined and solved creatively. This perspective has fueled my work as a teacher, leader, and advocate for equity in education.

The heart of this book lies in the stories, strategies, and successes I have witnessed and contributed to over decades in education. Whether working to redesign schools through bold initiatives like the XQ+RI Challenge, supporting incarcerated youth to reengage with their education, or collaborating with communities to develop career-readiness pipelines, I have learned that change is never linear. Progress is iterative, often requiring us to pause, reflect, and pivot, just as I did when I first learned to read.

This playbook is not about prescribing a single path. Instead, it offers a framework rooted in Implementation Science, a discipline that emphasizes planning, execution, monitoring, and continuous assessment. These stages are informed by research and practice but brought to life through real-world applications that recognize the diversity and context of schools, students, and communities.

Change, as I've learned, is often messy and unpredictable. It demands that we confront hard truths about equity, access, and outcomes. Implementation Science equips us to navigate this complexity with intention and rigor. By focusing on process as much as outcomes, the framework ensures that our efforts are ambitious and sustainable. This is crucial in education, where quick fixes rarely address the systemic challenges that underlie student achievement gaps. Instead, we must commit to reflective, data-driven, and adaptive strategies.

My journey to this work has been shaped by personal and professional experiences that taught me the value of persistence, empathy, and collaboration. As a child who struggled to read, I learned early on that success requires determination and creative problem-solving. Later, as an educator and leader, I saw how these lessons applied to larger systems. I witnessed the transformative power of relationships, whether between teacher and student, leader and faculty, district to site, or school and community. These relationships are the bedrock of effective implementation, ensuring that all voices are heard and valued.

Throughout this book, you will find not only frameworks and tools but also stories that illustrate how the process unfolds in real-world contexts. From rural districts working to align curriculum with high-demand career fields to urban schools striving to close equity gaps, these examples highlight the importance of context. Successful implementation is never one-size-fits-all; it is tailored, iterative, and deeply connected to the unique needs of each learning community. The stories in this playbook are a testament to the creativity and resilience of educators, leaders, and students who refuse to settle for anything less than excellence.

Leadership is at the core of implementation. Reflecting on the mentors and colleagues who have shaped my career, I am reminded that leadership is not about commanding authority but about serving with humility and purpose. In this book, I draw upon lessons from inspiring figures—teachers who empowered their students, principals who transformed struggling schools, and district leaders who championed equity with courage. Their stories remind us that leadership is not a position but a practice grounded in a relentless focus on student success.

This playbook is also a call to action. The challenges facing education today are formidable: persistent achievement gaps, teacher burnout, resource inequities, and the evolving demands of the 21st-century workforce. Yet within these challenges lie tremendous opportunities to innovate, to reimagine what is possible, and to build systems that truly serve all learners. Implementation Science provides a road map for this work, guiding leaders through the steps of planning, implementation, monitoring, and assessment with clarity and purpose.

As you engage with this playbook, I invite you to see it as more than a guide. It is an invitation to lead with courage, embrace complexity, and center the voices of those we serve. The work of education is about transformation—not only of systems but also of the individuals within them, including ourselves. This transformation requires us to be vulnerable, to question our assumptions, and to persist even when progress feels slow or elusive. In this space of discomfort and discovery, meaningful change takes root.

The journey to authentic leadership and impactful change often feels as it did for me, upside down and backward. Yet, it is precisely in this space that we find the greatest opportunity to grow. Together, let us build schools where every student is empowered to learn, every teacher equipped to succeed, and every leader inspired to serve. Through the lens of Implementation Science, we can reimagine education as a system that works for all—a system where equity is not an aspiration but a reality.

—Dr. Julia Carlson

INTRODUCTION

The challenges facing schools and districts today demand more than incremental improvements; they require comprehensive turnarounds driven by focused, strategic changes in practice and policy. *Implementation Science: A Playbook for Instructional Leaders* is designed as a practical guide to help educators navigate the complexities of educational reform and achieve lasting change. This book combines the rigor of Implementation Science with actionable strategies. It provides a step-by-step framework for school and district leaders committed to transforming their institutions with thought-provoking questions to consider with your instructional team.

Improving student outcomes often starts with strategic planning and choosing evidence-based curricula, interventions, and practices—but it doesn't end there. Interventions must be implemented with integrity to ensure the efficacy of programs and systems. As a nation, we have moved past the general checklist of fidelity checks. This playbook is the first on applying Implementation Science—an evidence-based framework for bridging the research-*to*-practice—to school and district turnaround.

This essential playbook will help ensure that the appropriate interventions are planned for, selected, implemented, monitored, and assessed so they help as many children as possible. Administrators, researchers, and policymakers will examine how the growing field of Implementation Science can help close the research-*to*-practice gap by focusing in on the bridge of "***to***." Readers will discover:

- The core components needed to implement and sustain programs with specific tools and resources to incorporate within their practice.
- Explore specific examples of how to build practitioner competency and promote high-fidelity implementation to ensure increased accountability scores.
- Understand how to create readiness for change and why it's so important.

- Get in-depth guidance on strategic planning and scaling programs at the school and district.
- Gain access to tools and resources for the three components of Implementation Science to support turnaround.
- See how Implementation Science can inform the process of systems change for school and district turnaround.

More than a playbook for effective implementation and scale-up, this volume addresses the theoretical foundation of the stages of Implementation Science grounded in school and district turnaround. In addition, we will explore the impact of Implementation Science on research, practice, and policy implications in a post-COVID world.

Science of Reading–based core curriculum will serve as the foundational intervention for grounding the principles of Implementation Science throughout this book. Drawing on decades of research from cognitive science, linguistics, and education, the Science of Reading emphasizes evidence-based instructional practices that focus on developing phonemic awareness, phonics, fluency, vocabulary, and comprehension. By aligning the structured, systematic approach of the Science of Reading with the rigorous framework of Implementation Science, this book aims to provide educational leaders with a strategic pathway for adopting, scaling, and sustaining effective reading instruction. The intersection of these two fields ensures that best practices in reading are being implemented, and they are done with fidelity, using continuous improvement cycles, data-driven decisions, and stakeholder engagement to achieve lasting, meaningful outcomes in literacy for all students.

A foundational volume on Implementation Science for leaders, this book will help improve long-term outcomes for all students. Leaders will learn how to replicate and sustain best practices, researchers will be ready to conduct more informed program evaluations, and policymakers will discover what it really takes to have effective, sustainable programs and systems.

Why Implementation Science?

Implementation Science is the study of methods to promote the systematic uptake of research findings and other evidence-based practices into routine practice. In the context of education, it offers a structured approach to applying proven strategies in new settings, ensuring that innovations are effectively integrated and sustained over time. As Fixsen, Naoom, Blase, Friedman, and Wallace (2005) articulate, "Effective implementation processes are the missing link between the promise of evidence-based education and the realization of its powerful effects in everyday practice" (p. 12).

This discipline is particularly crucial in educational turnarounds, where the stakes are high and the need for rapid, substantial improvement is urgent. Utilizing Implementation Science, leaders can more effectively translate what works from research *to* practice, ensuring that change initiatives not only start strong but also have the resilience to last.

The Structure of This Playbook

This playbook is structured to guide you through the entire process, from the initial planning stages to the long-term sustainment of new practices:

1. **Education Now:** A look at key education legislation shaping public education. In 2024, American education stands at a critical juncture, shaped by a convergence of challenges and opportunities that have redefined the landscape for school and district leaders. As we reflect on the current state of education, it becomes evident that several key themes and trends are influencing policies, practices, and outcomes across the nation.
2. **Understanding the Foundation:** We begin with an exploration of the key principles of Implementation Science and their relevance to education. This section sets the foundation for the strategies discussed throughout the book, emphasizing the importance of evidence-based practices.

3. **Preparation for Change:** The third section addresses the crucial preparation phase, where leaders assess their readiness for change, identify the necessary resources, and engage stakeholders. As Fullan (2007) notes, "Change is a process, not an event."
4. **Initiating Implementation:** Here, we delve into the strategies for initiating change, including the selection of appropriate interventions, their adaptation to fit local contexts, and the early stages of implementation. The focus is on practical actions that can be taken to start the transformation process effectively.
5. **Monitoring Progress and Adapting Strategies:** This section covers ongoing assessment and adaptation. Leaders will learn how to establish robust monitoring systems and use data to continuously adapt strategies. Kouzes and Posner (2017) emphasize the role of leaders in this process: "Leaders turn challenges into successes by constantly monitoring their progress and adjusting their behaviors."
6. **Sustaining and Scaling Up Success:** The final section focuses on how to sustain and scale successful practices. It guides embedding successful changes into the school culture and expanding them to a broader context. This is where the long-term impact of turnaround efforts is solidified.

Who Should Read This Book?

Implementation Science: A Playbook for Instructional Leaders is intended for school and district leaders—principals, superintendents, curriculum coordinators, and anyone involved in school improvement efforts—who are looking for a systematic approach to leading significant instructional change. Additionally, policymakers, educational consultants, and scholars will find valuable insights into the practical application of Implementation Science in academic settings.

With *Implementation Science: A Playbook for Instructional Leaders*, you hold not just a book but a blueprint for action. This guide is crafted to support you in translating the potential of educational research into the reality of improved school performance, ensuring that every student benefits from high-quality education. As you turn these pages, you will be equipped with knowledge and the tools and confidence to lead and sustain meaningful change in your schools and districts.

Bibliography

Fixsen, D. L., Naoom, S. F., Blase, K. A., Friedman, R. M., & Wallace, F. (2005). Implementation research: A synthesis of the literature. *University of South Florida, Louis de la Parte Florida Mental Health Institute, The National Implementation Research Network.*

Fullan, M. (2007). *The new meaning of educational change.* Teachers College Press.

Kouzes, J. M., & Posner, B. Z. (2017). *The leadership challenge: How to make extraordinary things happen in organizations.* Jossey-Bass.

PART I

Current State of Education

The field of public, charter, and private education is constantly evolving, shaped by societal needs, technological advancements, and educational research that result in legislative actions that respond to them. The following is a brief overview of public education in the United States, highlighting key legislation that significantly impacts how education is delivered and assessed. It explores both historical and recent legislative acts, examining their intentions, implementations, and the outcomes they have driven.

Turnaround strategies have largely addressed critical tools in addressing the challenges underperforming schools and districts face. These efforts focus on restructuring and revitalizing school systems to improve student outcomes, often due to chronic underperformance and in the context of state-mandated or federally mandated interventions. The key elements of successful turnaround efforts encompass leadership changes, rigorous data-driven instruction, enhanced teacher support and development, and active community engagement. By leveraging targeted resources and tailored solutions, turnaround initiatives aim to disrupt patterns of chronic underachievement, fostering sustainable improvements in academic performance.

CHAPTER ONE

Historical Context

Efforts aimed at fostering equality, ensuring access, and promoting excellence have continuously shaped education legislation in the United States. The historical and current legislative landscape is essential for educational leaders to understand as they seek to implement meaningful change.

For the past two decades, turnaround strategies have been one of America's solutions to fixing its struggling schools and districts. These are not new strategies; they usually arise as a response to accountability ratings, and they attempt to "turnaround" leadership, improve instructional practice, and skyrocket overall accountability. The increased use of these interventions can mainly be attributed to accountability-related pressures that in part are due to No Child Left Behind (NCLB) as well as its successor, Every Student Succeeds Act (ESSA). Neither law even attempted data-driven accountability, revealing long-term underperformance and compelling interventions to counter instructional collapse

It is not unusual for turnaround strategies to involve things like leadership turnover, curriculum overhauls, and extensive professional development. In a few cases, entire districts have been seized by the state in order to spur more aggressive implementation. These plans aim at achieving rapid improvement in student performance, based on what is proven to work best for students starting out further behind—especially strategies targeting disadvantaged schools. There have been some success stories, as in Massachusetts's Lawrence Public Schools (which we will explore more later), but the record is decidedly mixed. Indeed, critics point out that many turnarounds don't actually fix the problems of poverty and lack of resources, potentially perpetuating such cycles by focusing on short-term gains as a quick fix. Yet this paradigm of taking schools over and "turning them around" continues to predominate as the conversation persists among educational leaders about how to improve our poorest-performing campuses through a model that marries accountability with well-intentioned assistance.

Elementary and Secondary Education Act of 1965

It goes back to 1965 when our nation made a collective decision, through the passage of the Elementary and Secondary Education Act (ESEA), to fundamentally change its approach. Central to President Lyndon B. Johnson's War on Poverty, this historic legislation sought to provide equal access to quality education for all children, regardless of family income or social status. This was a major project for Johnson, who believed education was key to promoting social mobility and justice. The shift away from local control in public education took place with the passage of this landmark law—the ESEA. The legislation aimed to close achievement gaps that had left many students, particularly those in poverty and other disadvantaged groups, behind.

The ESEA was designed to provide a new vision for public education, specifically addressing the needs of America's disadvantaged and at-risk children. It provided grants for K-12 education with a preference for high-poverty areas. For the first time, schools received extra help to better close educational gaps and allow poor students to succeed as well.

Klein (2015) described the ESEA as a significant federal education policy that opened up educational opportunities for all children. This bill set the stage for further reforms by promoting accountability and equitable educational outcomes. Over the years, reauthorizations of ESEA continued to refine its goals and keep the focus on ensuring that all students can succeed academically.

The Individuals with Disabilities Education Act

The passage of the Education for All Handicapped Children Act in 1975, now known as the Individuals with Disabilities Education Act (IDEA), one this author is very familiar with from serving as a special education teacher, represents another critical milestone in educational equity. IDEA was designed to ensure students with disabilities can access free and appropriate public education (FAPE). Before this law, students with disabilities were often excluded from the classroom and denied opportunities for academic and personal growth.

IDEA ensures that schools accommodate the individual needs of students with disabilities and prepare them for life beyond school, including employment and independent living. "IDEA ensures that all children with disabilities are entitled to a free appropriate public education to meet their unique needs and prepare them for further education, employment, and independent living" (Yell, 2019). This legislation fundamentally changed the way schools approach special education, requiring individualized education programs (IEPs) and providing federal funds to support students' needs.

IDEA has had a profound impact on school practices, ensuring that students with disabilities are included in general education settings whenever appropriate. The law also guarantees that parents of children with disabilities have a voice in educational decision-making and access to resources that can help them advocate for their child's educational rights.

The No Child Left Behind Act of 2001

The No Child Left Behind Act (NCLB), enacted in 2001 under President George W. Bush, reauthorized the ESEA with a new focus on accountability. NCLB mandated that states establish academic standards and assess student progress through standardized testing. Schools were required to report annual performance data and face penalties if they failed to meet progress goals. NCLB also aimed to close achievement gaps by holding schools accountable for the performance of all students, including historically underserved populations. This act is of particular note as strategic planning became commonplace in districts who were marked as chronically underperforming and led to a rise in external consultants being contracted to support leaders.

"NCLB aimed to provide parents with data on school effectiveness and make schools accountable for student outcomes" (Hess &

Petrilli, 2006). While NCLB sparked controversy over its emphasis on standardized testing and punitive measures for underperforming schools, it nevertheless highlighted the need for data-driven decision-making and accountability in education.

NCLB's legacy lies in its emphasis on ensuring that all students, regardless of background, have access to high-quality education and that schools are held accountable for student performance. Despite its eventual replacement, the themes of accountability and equity from NCLB continue to shape education policy today.

Every Student Succeeds Act of 2015

The Every Student Succeeds Act (ESSA) of 2015 was a response to the criticisms of NCLB, offering states more autonomy in setting their educational goals while maintaining a focus on underserved populations. ESSA shifted control of accountability systems from the federal government to states, allowing them to develop tailored approaches to school improvement and assessment. States employed entire departments to "transformation" and/or "turnaround."

"ESSA was signed to reauthorize the 1965 ESEA, thereby replacing NCLB and returning accountability and school improvement decisions back to the states" (Murphy, 2016, p. 114). The law reflects a recognition that states are better positioned to address the unique needs of their schools and students, while still upholding federal requirements to ensure educational equity.

ESSA also promotes evidence-based interventions and places an increased focus on nonacademic indicators of school success, such as school climate and student engagement. This law encourages a more holistic approach to education, one that extends beyond test scores. However, the pandemic in 2020 disrupted educational systems globally, leading to school closures, remote learning, and significant learning loss, particularly among marginalized communities. During the pandemic, states received waivers from federal testing requirements, and many of ESSA's accountability measures were temporarily suspended. After COVID-19, schools faced heightened challenges in addressing the widened achievement gaps and the social-emotional needs of students.

Recent research indicates that early literacy scores have remained relatively stagnant over the past several decades, even through the disruptions caused by COVID-19. A 2023 report from the National Assessment of Educational Progress (NAEP) highlighted that reading scores for 13-year-olds have shown little significant improvement since the 1970s, with no substantial changes even following the pandemic. While the pandemic exacerbated learning challenges in many areas, the long-standing issues in literacy education appear largely unaffected by the crisis, underscoring the need for deeper systemic changes.

The Response to Federal and State Legislation: The Rise of State Takeover

State takeover of chronically underperforming school districts has long been promoted as a strategy to reverse academic decline and improve student outcomes. Proponents argue that state intervention can support districts and schools by bringing much-needed leadership, resources, and reforms to struggling schools. However, the evidence supporting the effectiveness of state receivership remains mixed, with several cases showing little to no improvement in academic achievement despite years of state control.

The Promise of State Takeovers

State takeovers, often initiated when local districts fail to meet performance benchmarks, are based on the premise that state authorities, removed from local political pressures, can implement the bold changes necessary to improve struggling schools. Advocates for receivership assert that the state can introduce a more rigorous focus on accountability, bring in new leadership, and inject additional funding where needed.

One of the more notable examples of a state takeover is the intervention in the Lawrence Public Schools (LPS) in Massachusetts, which began in 2012, and the site in which this author studied and completed their dissertation. At the time, Lawrence was one of the lowest-performing districts in the state. The Massachusetts Department of Elementary and Secondary Education, with the state-appointed receiver Jeff Riley, implemented significant reforms, including extending the school day, increasing instructional time, and hiring new leadership. These efforts led to some measurable improvements. According to a study conducted by Schueler, Goodman, and Deming (2017), Lawrence saw gains in student achievement, particularly in math and English Language Arts (ELA), with state data showing an increase in the number of students performing at proficient levels. However, Lawrence's experience represents an outlier in the broader landscape of state takeovers, where successes are rare and incremental at best. While Lawrence provides a model for what can be achieved under ideal conditions, other districts have struggled to replicate this success. The success under Jeff Riley propelled him to Commissioner of the Massachusetts Department of Elementary and Secondary Education.

Despite isolated successes like Lawrence, the overall track record of state takeovers is underwhelming. A comprehensive study conducted in 2021 by Beth Schueler, an assistant professor at the University of Virginia, and Joshua Bleiberg of the Annenberg Institute at Brown University, examined 35 school districts across 14 states that had been placed under state control. Their findings were stark: "Overall, we find no evidence that state takeover improves academic achievement" (Schueler & Bleiberg, 2021, p. 162). This sobering conclusion has cast doubt on the effectiveness of state receivership as a long-term solution for underperforming districts.

The case of Holyoke Public Schools in Massachusetts highlights the limitations of state intervention, even when it is the same state with a successful takeover. Holyoke was placed under state control in 2015, and nearly a decade later, the district remains mired in poor performance. In 2023, only 6% of students in grades 3 to 8 were proficient in math, and just 9% were proficient in English, representing a significant decline from prepandemic levels (Jonas, 2024). Despite improvements in graduation rates and increased access to early education, basic academic outcomes have stagnated, leading many to question whether state intervention has made a meaningful difference in the lives of students or whether the impact of solid leadership is the most important factor.

Michael Moriarty, a member of the Massachusetts Board of Education, acknowledged these challenges: "The state owns the outcomes at this point. It does raise questions about the efficacy of this tool" (Jonas, 2024). Moriarty's statement reflects a growing sentiment among education stakeholders that while state takeovers can bring organizational changes and temporary boosts in certain areas, they often fail to address the root causes of academic underperformance.

Finally, in 2019, the Rhode Island Department of Education (RIDE) took the unprecedented step of assuming control of the Providence Public School District (PPSD) following a devastating report from Johns Hopkins University. The report highlighted that the district had been underperforming for over 20 years. Chronic underperformance was entrenched across multiple levels, from administrative inefficiencies to a lack of basic instructional resources. At the time, Rhode Island Governor Gina Raimondo described the state of Providence schools as "devastating" and committed to drastic action to rectify the situation (Johns Hopkins University, 2019, pp. 2–3). It pointed to systemic failures in student achievement, school culture, and governance, showing that problems had been persistent and were compounded over many years, under many superintendents, well before the COVID-19 pandemic exacerbated the situation.

The state's intervention, led by Education Commissioner Angélica Infante-Green, was billed as a necessary turnaround effort for a system that had long failed its students, regardless of it being unsupported by research. However, nearly 5 years later, the promised improvements in student performance have largely failed to materialize, again raising serious questions about the efficacy of state takeovers in education.

From the outset, the state takeover was seen as a bold experiment in school reform, as Infante-Green's vision included high expectations for academic achievement, new leadership structures, and improved teacher recruitment and retention. "We knew this would not be an easy process, but our goal was clear: to provide every student in Providence with the quality education they deserve," Infante-Green stated at the start of the takeover (The 74 Million, 2024).

Despite these ambitious goals, implementation challenges have persisted. Teacher turnover remains high, and while there have been some improvements in school infrastructure, these have not translated into significant gains in student performance. According to a 2024 report by SchoolWorks, which evaluated the state's intervention, student outcomes in core subjects like ELA and mathematics remain well below the targets set by the turnaround plan. "None of the RICAS scores, except third grade math, were on track with the turnaround plan," the report noted, underscoring the lack of progress across multiple grade levels (SchoolWorks, 2024, p. 6). As of 2023, fewer than 20% of students in Providence were proficient in these subjects, a statistic that has remained relatively unchanged since the takeover began (Russo, 2023).

"We expected to see a significant turnaround, but the results just haven't been there," said a Providence School Board member in 2024, adding that the board is now pushing for the return of local control by 2025 (*Providence Journal*, 2023). The lack of improvement has led to frustration among parents, educators, and local officials alike. The state takeover, which was initially greeted with cautious optimism, is now viewed by many as having failed to live up to its promises.

One major issue that has hindered progress is the district's persistent struggle with teacher retention and morale. High teacher turnover rates, a problem flagged in the Johns Hopkins report, have not improved significantly under state control. "The consistent churn in staff makes it incredibly difficult to build the sustained progress that students need," said a Providence teacher in a *Providence Journal*, 2023 interview. This instability has directly impacted classroom learning and the ability to implement new curricula effectively.

Despite the lack of academic progress, some positive developments have occurred during the state's intervention. According to the SchoolWorks report, "students are feeling an increased 'sense of belonging,' 17 percentage points higher in the 2022-2023 school year than in 2020-2021" (SchoolWorks, 2024, p. 8). School facilities, which were in dire condition, have also seen improvements.

However, these gains have done little to offset the stagnation in academic achievement, which is an accountability measure.

The state's efforts to address systemic inequities through new leadership and resource allocation have been hampered by persistent financial constraints. The City of Providence has been criticized for failing to meet its obligations under the Crowley Act, which mandates increased municipal investment in education. These financial shortfalls have limited the effectiveness of the state's intervention and contributed to the ongoing struggles within the district (The 74 Million, 2024).

The state takeover of Providence Public Schools was initiated to transform a deeply dysfunctional district. As the debate over the district's future continues, Providence's experience raises important questions about the effectiveness of state takeovers as a tool for educational reform. Without significant improvements in academic outcomes, the ultimate success of the state's intervention remains in doubt.

Several factors contribute to the limited success of state takeovers. One significant issue is the lack of sustained local support and community engagement. State interventions can sometimes alienate local stakeholders, including school boards—which often become voiceless in a takeover—teachers' unions, and parents, leading to resistance and mistrust.

Another challenge is resource constraints. This was a key finding in the study by Schueler and Bleiberg, which noted that state takeovers rarely resulted in the necessary long-term financial commitment to support deep and lasting reforms (Schueler & Bleiberg, 2021). Many underperforming districts are in low-income areas with limited funding and inadequate infrastructure. State intervention alone often cannot resolve these systemic issues. Academic progress remains elusive without sufficient investment in teacher development, school facilities, and student support services.

Given the mixed results of state takeovers, many education experts and policymakers call for reevaluating the model. Some argue that state intervention should be more collaborative, emphasizing partnering with local leaders rather than replacing them. Others suggest that state takeovers should be viewed as temporary measures, with clearly defined goals and exit strategies to return control to local authorities once improvements are made.

The case of Holyoke illustrates this evolving perspective. After 9 years of state receivership, Massachusetts officials are now preparing to return control of the district to local hands. "We are officially entering the transition process to return to local control," announced acting state education commissioner Russell Johnston in 2024 (Jonas, 2024). This decision reflects the growing recognition that while state takeovers can play a role in stabilizing struggling districts, they are not a panacea and must be accompanied by broader, more systemic reforms.

State takeovers of underperforming school districts have shown limited success in improving academic outcomes. While examples like Lawrence Public Schools offer some hope, the overall evidence suggests that state receivership is not a guaranteed solution for chronically low-performing districts. Challenges such as insufficient resources, lack of community engagement, and the complex nature of educational reform have hindered the effectiveness of these interventions. As policymakers continue to explore ways to support struggling schools, it is clear that any strategy must be comprehensive, involving not only state oversight but also local collaboration, sustained investment, and a commitment to addressing the underlying inequities that contribute to educational failure.

The Impact of Legislation on Educational Practices

The legislative acts discussed in this chapter have had far-reaching implications for educational practices in schools across the United States. These laws have influenced curriculum design, professional development, and efforts to promote educational equity.

- **Curriculum and Assessment:** Laws such as ESSA have prompted schools to develop curricula that are inclusive of diverse perspectives and responsive to the needs of all students. This has led to more culturally responsive teaching practices and a broader emphasis on critical thinking and problem-solving skills.
- **Professional Development:** Legislative mandates focusing on teacher quality have led to enhanced professional development programs, particularly in the areas of diversity, technology

integration, and differentiated instruction. These programs aim to equip teachers with the skills needed to meet the demands of a changing educational landscape.
- **Educational Equity:** IDEA, ESSA, and other laws have played pivotal roles in promoting educational equity. These laws mandate that schools meet the needs of all students, regardless of ability, race, or socioeconomic status. This has driven schools to adopt more inclusive practices and focus on closing achievement gaps.

Questions for Reflection

To deepen your understanding of the current legislative environment and its impact on education, consider the following questions:

1. How have laws like ESEA and IDEA shaped the role of federal and state governments in education?
2. In what ways do the policies of NCLB and ESSA differ in their approaches to accountability and student assessment?
3. How have these laws influenced the design and implementation of curricula in K-12 schools? Consider how the curriculum has evolved to be more inclusive and responsive to student diversity.
4. What role does professional development play in ensuring teachers can effectively implement the changes mandated by recent education legislation?

By reflecting on these questions, educational leaders can better understand the legislative context in which they operate and consider how these laws impact their practice.

Bibliography

Hess, F. M., & Petrilli, M. J. (2006). *No Child Left Behind: A primer*. Peter Lang.

Johns Hopkins University School of Education. (2019). *An independent review of the Providence Public School District*. Johns Hopkins University.

Jonas, M. (2024, April 3). *State exit from Holyoke puts spotlight on mixed takeover record: Researchers find more positive outcomes in Lawrence, Springfield*. CommonWealth Beacon. https://commonwealthbeacon.org/education/state-exit-from-holyoke-puts-spotlight-on-underwhelming-takeover-record/

Klein, A. (2015). The history of ESEA: Federal education legislation's impact on schools. *Education Week, 35*(6), 10–15.

Murphy, J. (2016). Reconsidering the federal role in education. *Peabody Journal of Education, 91*(3), 389–402.

Russo, A. (2023, June 16). Providence public school day for 2023-2024 school year will be longer. *The Providence Journal.* https://www.providencejournal.com/story/news/education/2023/06/16/providence-public-school-day-for-2023-2024-school-year-will-be-longer/70329431007/?utm_source=chatgpt.com

Schueler, B. E., & Bleiberg, J. (2021). The effectiveness of state takeovers in education reform. *Educational Policy Review, 12*(4), 489–506.

Schueler, B. E., Goodman, J. S., & Deming, D. J. (2017). Can states take over and turn around school districts? Evidence from Lawrence, Massachusetts. *Educational Evaluation and Policy Analysis, 39*(2), 311–332. https://doi.org/10.3102/0162373716685824

SchoolWorks. (2024, August). Local Education Agency Review Report: RIDE LEA Review of Providence Public School District. *Rhode Island Department of Education.*

The 74 Million. (2024). *Progress and challenges in Providence Public School turnaround efforts.* https://www.the74million.org/article/rhode-island-to-keep-control-of-providence-schools-for-three-more-years/

Yell, M. L. (2019). *The law and special education* (5th ed.). Pearson.

CHAPTER TWO

A Contextual Approach: A Look at the Science of Reading

There has been a significant shift in how educators approach reading instruction in recent years, primarily driven by advances in cognitive science and educational research. This "Science of Reading" refers to the study of how children learn to read and effective teaching practices. Legislation reflecting this knowledge aims to ensure that reading instruction in public schools is grounded in this evidence-based approach.

In the following chapters, we will explore the use of Implementation Science through early literacy curriculum selection and implementation. Though interventions in school systems are vast, the "Reading Wars" have highlighted many aspects we will explore and thus provide a natural avenue to understand this new framework better.

Understanding the Science of Reading

The Science of Reading refers to a comprehensive body of research from various fields, including cognitive psychology, education, linguistics, and neuroscience, focused on how children acquire reading skills. This research identifies five key components of effective reading instruction:

1. **Phonemic Awareness:** The ability to hear, identify, and manipulate individual sounds (phonemes) in spoken words.
2. **Phonics:** Understanding the relationship between sounds and their written representations (letters and letter combinations).
3. **Fluency:** The ability to read text accurately, quickly, and with appropriate expression.

4. **Vocabulary:** Knowledge of word meanings is essential for spoken and written language comprehension.
5. **Comprehension:** The ability to understand and interpret what is being read.

"Effective reading instruction must be comprehensive and include these essential components to support all aspects of literacy" (Seidenberg, 2017, p. 254). The Science of Reading underscores the importance of explicit, systematic instruction in these areas, particularly in the early grades, to lay a solid foundation for future reading success.

Historical Context

The debate over reading instruction has a long history in the United States, marked by a pendulum swing between phonics-based and whole-language approaches. Phonics-based instruction focuses on teaching the relationships between letters and sounds, while whole-language instruction emphasizes reading comprehension and exposure to rich, authentic literature.

A significant turning point came with the publication of the National Reading Panel's report in 2000, which synthesized decades of research and called for a balanced approach that includes explicit instruction in phonemic awareness and phonics, as well as fluency, vocabulary, and comprehension. "The report underscored the necessity of phonics and other foundational skills in early reading instruction" (National Reading Panel, 2000, p. 12). This report provided the foundation for subsequent educational policies and legislation centered around the Science of Reading.

A pivotal moment came years later with the release of two influential podcasts: *The Right to Read* and *Sold a Story*. These series ignited national conversations about the shortcomings of traditional reading instruction methods and underscored the urgency of adopting evidence-based practices. The accessibility of these podcasts reached households nationwide in a way research often failed. These podcasts also brought to light the personal struggle of families when children failed to learn to read in elementary school.

The Right to Read, which premiered alongside a documentary in 2023, presented stories of children who struggled with reading due to ineffective instructional programs. It demonstrated how structured literacy, emphasizing phonics and direct instruction, could reverse these challenges. The documentary highlighted the advocacy work of individuals like Kareem Weaver, who argued that structured literacy is essential for equitable education, particularly for underserved students (MacKenzie, 2023). The series helped amplify the Science of Reading movement by connecting personal narratives of struggle with a broader push for systemic educational reform.

Similarly, *Sold a Story*, released in 2022, offered an investigative examination of how discredited reading methods—such as whole language and balanced literacy—became entrenched in U.S. schools despite decades of cognitive science research showing their ineffectiveness (Hanford, 2022). The podcast revealed these approaches' harmful effects on millions of students' literacy development, leading to a widespread literacy crisis. Following the release of *Sold a Story*, at least 15 states revised their reading instruction laws and practices, embedding the Science of Reading as a cornerstone of their educational policies (Hanford, 2022).

Both podcasts have transformed how educators and policymakers approach reading instruction. They emphasize the need for structured, research-backed methods to tackle the nation's literacy challenges effectively.

Recent Legislation Influenced by the Science of Reading

Recent legislation across the United States has been significantly influenced by the Science of Reading. It reflects a shift toward evidence-based literacy instruction that prioritizes phonics, direct instruction, and structured approaches over previously popular methods like balanced literacy. These legislative changes have been driven by a growing recognition of the importance of early reading proficiency, grounded in cognitive science research that emphasizes how children learn to read.

At the federal level, the Comprehensive Literacy State Development (CLSD) grants, funded through the Every Student Succeeds Act

(ESSA), support state and local efforts to improve literacy instruction based on evidence from the Science of Reading. These grants encourage states to develop comprehensive literacy plans, previously reserved for schools and districts in turnaround, focusing on underserved populations and promoting early literacy through structured, explicit instruction (U.S. Department of Education, 2020). Many states receiving CLSD grants have restructured their literacy programs to align more closely with research-driven practices.

These legislative efforts demonstrate a growing national consensus that the Science of Reading should guide literacy instruction. By aligning laws and policies with decades of research on reading acquisition, states are working to ensure that students, particularly those at risk of falling behind, receive the support they need to achieve literacy success.

"Federal funding through grants like CLSD underscores the national priority on effective literacy instruction based on the best available evidence" (U.S. Department of Education, 2020). This support allows states to implement comprehensive literacy plans that address the needs of students at various stages of development, from early childhood through adolescence.

State-Level Initiatives

In response to growing concerns about low literacy rates and persistent achievement gaps, several states have enacted legislation that requires reading instruction to align with the Science of Reading. These laws typically mandate specific teacher training and emphasize explicit phonics instruction as part of comprehensive literacy education.

For example, Arkansas passed the Right to Read Act, which mandates that educators receive professional development in evidence-based reading instruction (Arkansas Department of Education, 2019). Similarly, Mississippi and North Carolina have enacted laws requiring schools to adopt instructional practices rooted in the Science of Reading. These legislative efforts ensure that all students, particularly those struggling with literacy, receive instruction grounded in the best available research.

Similarly, Mississippi's focus on reading reform has shown remarkable results. The state enacted the Literacy-Based Promotion Act in 2013, requiring third-grade students to demonstrate reading proficiency before advancing to the next grade. In 2021, the law was strengthened by further aligning instructional practices with the Science of Reading, mandating additional teacher training, and implementing interventions based on phonics and decoding skills (Mississippi Department of Education, 2021). As a result, Mississippi saw significant improvements in literacy outcomes, with reading scores improving at a faster rate than in most other states (Loewus, 2020).

"These laws reflect a legislative commitment to improving literacy through scientifically validated instructional methods" (Hanford, 2023). State-level initiatives are designed to provide a clear and consistent framework for schools, ensuring teachers have the knowledge and tools to implement effective reading instruction.

Implications for Educational Practice

The shift toward legislation influenced by the Science of Reading has significant implications for educational practice, particularly in how reading instruction is delivered, how teachers are trained, and how schools assess and support students struggling with literacy. These changes underscore a movement from outdated, less effective instructional methods toward practices rooted in decades of cognitive science research, which has demonstrated that explicit, systematic instruction in phonics, phonemic awareness, and decoding is critical for early reading success.

Curriculum and Instructional Changes

One of the primary implications for educational practice is restructuring curricula to align with the Science of Reading. This approach emphasizes explicit instruction in phonics and phonemic awareness, replacing balanced literacy models that previously dominated U.S. classrooms. Studies show that structured literacy programs are particularly effective for students with learning disabilities and those who struggle with reading acquisition (Kilpatrick, 2015). States like Mississippi, where new legislation has mandated Science of Reading-aligned curricula, have seen substantial gains in reading scores.

Perhaps one of the most important implications for educational practice is the focus on equity. The Science of Reading movement highlights the need to ensure all students, particularly those from historically underserved communities, receive high-quality reading instruction. By mandating evidence-based literacy practices and providing early interventions, these legislative efforts aim to close long-standing achievement gaps that have disproportionately affected students of color, low-income students, and students with disabilities (Shanahan, 2020).

The legislative shift toward the Science of Reading is reshaping educational practice across the United States, leading to significant changes in curriculum design, teacher training, assessment practices, and equity initiatives. By aligning instruction with evidence-based strategies, schools are better equipped to meet the diverse literacy needs of their students. As more states adopt these practices, the potential for widespread improvements in reading proficiency—and, ultimately, academic success—grows.

Administrator and Teacher Training

Another critical implication is the need for extensive administrator and teacher training. This shift recognizes that many educators previously lacked adequate training in phonics and other essential components of reading instruction, a gap that contributed to widespread literacy challenges (Moats, 2020). Educators nationwide must receive professional development, specific to their role, in the Science of Reading, ensuring they have the skills to implement research-based reading strategies in their classrooms.

This focus on professional development also extends to ongoing support and coaching for administrators and teachers, especially as they transition from older methods to new instructional practices. Continuous learning and skill refinement are critical, as research has shown that sustained professional development improves teacher efficacy and student outcomes in literacy (McKenna & Stahl, 2015).

This alignment between educator preparation, professional development, and classroom practice is crucial for successfully implementing Science of Reading legislation.

Assessment and Accountability

Many of the recent legislative acts include provisions related to assessment and accountability. Schools must regularly assess student progress using tools that reflect the Science of Reading, such as phonemic awareness and diagnostic reading assessments. These assessments help teachers identify struggling students and provide targeted interventions to support their learning. Regular, data-driven assessments are now required to monitor student progress and identify those at risk of falling behind. Early identification is crucial, as research demonstrates that the earlier reading difficulties are addressed, the more likely students are to overcome them (Kilpatrick, 2015).

Research shows that identifying reading difficulties by first or second grade, through reliable screening tools, allows for timely interventions that can significantly improve literacy outcomes. However, many assessments used in schools are not well aligned with the specific literacy curriculum in place. This misalignment makes it difficult to accurately evaluate a curriculum's effectiveness and identify students in need of support. When assessment tools do not match the instructional approaches or content taught, it can lead to misleading results and missed opportunities for intervention, further complicating efforts to improve literacy outcomes for all students. This disconnect between assessments and curriculum exacerbates the challenges in implementing evidence-based practices grounded in the Science of Reading.

The shift also emphasizes the importance of multi-tiered systems of support (MTSS), which provide varying levels of intervention depending on students' needs. MTSS frameworks ensure that struggling readers receive the appropriate level of support, ranging from classroom-based interventions to more intensive, individualized instruction for those with significant difficulties (Fuchs & Fuchs, 2017).

"Ongoing assessment is crucial for monitoring students' reading progress and ensuring that instruction meets their individual needs" (Kilpatrick, 2015, p. 222). The data gathered from these assessments inform instruction and serve as a tool for measuring the effectiveness of literacy programs at the school, district, and state levels.

Implementation Challenges

Despite the clear benefits of implementing the Science of Reading, schools and districts face significant challenges in practice. One of the primary challenges is resistance from educators who have been trained in or are more familiar with other methods of reading instruction and curriculum. Transitioning to new instructional practices often requires significant time, resources, and effort.

Additionally, providing new training, purchasing updated instructional materials and curriculum, and offering ongoing support and coaching can be prohibitive for many schools and districts, particularly those with limited budgets. "Effective implementation requires not only legislative action but also comprehensive support systems at all levels of education" (Wexler, 2020, pp. 15–32). Without this support, the potential impact of the legislation may be limited.

Another challenge that is less talked about is the site and district administration. Despite the growing emphasis on the Science of Reading in classroom instruction, there remains a significant gap in training for administrators. Many school leaders lack the knowledge necessary to support and sustain evidence-based reading practices within their schools. Research indicates that administrators may struggle to implement literacy initiatives effectively without adequate training, as they cannot provide the necessary guidance, resources, and oversight required for successful program execution (Maddox & Feng, 2021). Moreover, because school principals and district leaders play a critical role in setting instructional priorities and allocating professional development opportunities, their understanding of the Science of Reading is crucial for creating systemic change (Santoro, 2020). However, widespread inconsistencies in administrator preparation programs often leave them underequipped to support the transition from outdated reading methods to scientifically validated practices (Moats, 2020). As a result, even when teachers receive training in the Science of Reading, the lack of informed leadership at the administrative level can hinder the full implementation of effective literacy instruction.

Debates and Controversies

The shift toward the Science of Reading has sparked debate within the educational community. Critics argue that an overemphasis on phonics could overshadow other essential components of reading instruction, such as reading comprehension, critical thinking, and a love of reading. These critics caution that a balanced approach is necessary to ensure students develop comprehensive literacy skills.

One of the prevailing trends in education today is the continuous piling on of new responsibilities for teachers—without creating the necessary space for them to manage these additional tasks effectively. From new curriculum initiatives to the latest technological tools, the burden on teachers grows yearly. While these innovations are often introduced to improve student outcomes, they frequently come without the critical support or time for teachers to implement them effectively. As a result, teachers are forced to juggle many competing demands, leaving little room for them to focus on their core mission: teaching and fostering meaningful relationships with students.

This trend not only contributes to teacher burnout but also undermines the very improvements that these new initiatives are designed to achieve. When schools fail to provide teachers with the time, training, and resources they need, innovation becomes more of a hindrance than a help. Teachers are stretched thin, and the quality of instruction often suffers. Instead of being agents of change within the classroom, teachers are relegated to mere executors of an overwhelming checklist of tasks. The true potential of educational innovations can only be realized when schools create the space for teachers to master these tools and thoughtfully integrate them into their instructional practice.

Rather than constantly adding more to teachers' plates, schools must create environments where teachers have the time and mental space to collaborate, reflect, and engage deeply with their practice. This involves reducing unnecessary administrative tasks and ensuring that any new initiatives are carefully selected and supported. In doing so, schools can create a culture where innovation is sustainable and teachers are empowered to make meaningful, lasting impacts on their students' learning.

Balancing phonics instruction with other reading components is essential for developing comprehensive literacy skills. As educators implement Science of Reading practices, it is crucial to maintain a holistic view of literacy that includes foundational skills, higher-order thinking, and engagement with meaningful texts.

Conclusion

Legislation plays a pivotal role in shaping the policies and practices of public education, addressing emerging challenges, and ensuring that educational institutions serve all segments of society effectively. As the educational landscape continues to evolve, so will the legislative frameworks that govern it, requiring ongoing adaptation and commitment from educators, policymakers, and communities. Future legislative efforts must continue to balance flexibility with accountability, ensuring that all students receive the education they need to thrive in an increasingly complex world.

Recent legislation influenced by the Science of Reading represents a significant step toward improving literacy instruction based on robust educational research. As these laws are implemented across various states, ongoing evaluation and adaptation will be crucial to address challenges and ensure all students develop strong literacy skills.

Questions for Reflection

To deepen your understanding of recent legislation influenced by the Science of Reading, consider the following questions:

1. How has the Science of Reading shifted the approach to reading instruction in schools across the United States?

2. What are the key components of effective reading instruction as identified by the Science of Reading, and why are they important?
3. How have state-level initiatives such as the Right to Read Act in Arkansas and similar laws in other states addressed the challenges of improving literacy?
4. What role does federal support, such as the Comprehensive Literacy State Development (CLSD) grant program, play in advancing literacy initiatives nationwide?
5. What challenges might educators and schools face in implementing Science of Reading legislation, and how can these challenges be addressed?
6. How can schools balance phonics instruction and other crucial aspects of literacy, such as comprehension and engagement with texts?

Bibliography

Arkansas Department of Education. (2019). Right to Read Act. https://dese.ade.arkansas.gov

Fuchs, D., & Fuchs, L. S. (2017). Critique of the national evaluation of response to intervention: A case for simpler frameworks. *Exceptional Children, 83*(3), 255–268. https://doi.org/10.1177/0014402917693580

Hanford, E. (2019). Hard words: Why aren't kids being taught to read? *APM Reports.* https://www.apmreports.org/episode/2018/09/10/hard-words-why-american-kids-arent-being-taught-to-read

Hanford, E. (Producer). (2022). *Sold a story* [Podcast]. APM Reports, Minnesota Public Radio. https://www.apmreports.org

Kilpatrick, D. A. (2015). *Essentials of assessing, preventing, and overcoming reading difficulties.* Wiley.

Loewus, L. (2020, January 14). How Mississippi's approach to reading instruction is paying off. *Education Week.* https://www.edweek.org

Mackenzie, J. (Director). (2023). *The right to read* [Film]. Tribeca Films.

Maddox, K., & Feng, J. (2013). *Whole language instruction vs. phonics instruction: Effect on reading fluency and spelling accuracy of first grade students.* [Conference paper]. Annual Meeting of the Georgia Educational Research Association, Savannah, GA. https://eric.ed.gov/?id=ED545621

Maddox, A., & Feng, L. (2021). Leadership for literacy: The role of administrators in supporting effective reading instruction. *Journal of Educational Leadership, 45*(3), 180–195.

McKenna, M. C., & Stahl, K. A. D. (2015). *Assessment for reading instruction* (3rd ed.). Guilford Press.

Mississippi Department of Education. (2021). Literacy-Based Promotion Act update. https://www.mdek12.org

Moats, L. C. (2020). Speech to print: *Language essentials for teachers* (3rd ed.). Brookes Publishing.

National Reading Panel. (2000). *Teaching children to read: An evidence-based assessment of the scientific research literature on reading and its implications for reading instruction* (Reports of the subgroups). National Institute of Child Health and Human Development. https://www.nichd.nih.gov/sites/default/files/publications/pubs/nrp/Documents/report.pdf

Santoro, D. A. (2018). *Demoralized: Why teachers leave the profession they love and how they can stay*. Harvard Education Press.

Santoro, L. E. (2020). The critical role of leadership in literacy instruction: Supporting evidence-based practices. *Reading Research Quarterly, 55*(S1), S123–S136.

Seidenberg, M. S. (2017). *Language at the speed of sight: How we read, why so many can't, and what can be done about it*. Basic Books.

Shanahan, T. (2020). What constitutes evidence-based literacy instruction? *Reading Research Quarterly, 55*(S1), S361–S372.

U.S. Department of Education. (2020). Comprehensive literacy state development grants. https://www.ed.gov

Wexler, N. (2020). *The knowledge gap: The hidden cause of America's broken education system—and how to fix it*. Avery.

PART II

What Is Implementation Science, and Why Does it Matter in Education?

As Educational/Instructional Leaders, you play a pivotal role in shaping your students' future and supporting your administrators and teachers through meaningful change. Implementing a new intervention can feel like a daunting task. Implementation Science studies methods and strategies to promote adopting and integrating evidence-based practices, interventions, and policies into routine practice to improve health and education outcomes. This field is critical in bridging the gap between research *to* practice, ensuring that innovations are effectively translated into real-world settings and monitored and assessed for strategic impact. Effectively Implementation Science is the line between the buckets of work to ensure intended outcomes. This chapter explores the tenets of Implementation Science, its framework, and its key components, highlighting its significance in educational turnaround.

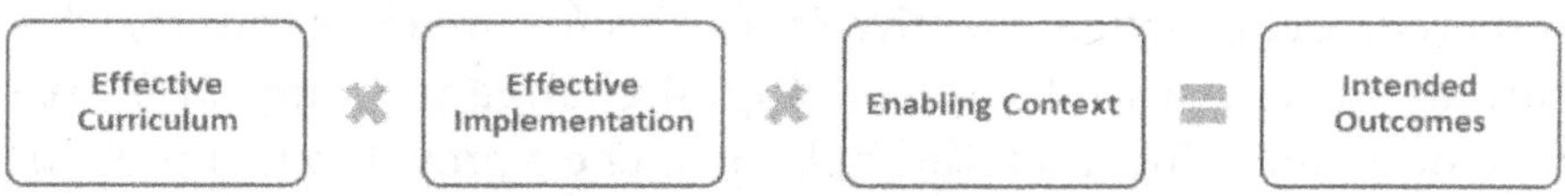

Figure II.1. IS Equation

Fixsen, D. L., & Blase, K. A. (2020). Active implementation frameworks. In P. Nilsen & S. A. Birken (Eds.), *Handbook on implementation science* (pp. 62–68). Edward Elgar Publishing.

Implementation Science operates through a holistic framework that focuses on three critical "buckets" essential for successful implementation: enabling context, effective intervention, and effective implementation. These buckets work together to ensure that evidence-based practices are planned for, adopted, sustained, and optimized for real-world use. Below, we will explore these buckets, drawing on our current understanding of the Science of Reading to highlight their significance.

The Interconnectedness of the Three Buckets

These three buckets are interconnected—effective intervention, effective implementation, and enabling context. An enabling context provides the foundation for efficacious interventions to be selected and implemented. Without a supportive context, even the most effective intervention may fail. Similarly, an intervention may have solid evidence behind it, but if it is not implemented effectively, its potential impact will be diminished.

"The success of implementation depends on the alignment and interaction of enabling contexts, effective interventions, and effective implementation practices" (Damschroder et al., 2009, p. 50). This interconnectedness highlights the need for a comprehensive approach to implementation, where each bucket is given the attention and resources required to ensure successful outcomes.

The three buckets of Implementation Science are essential to the successful adoption, integration, and sustainability of evidence-based practices in education. By ensuring that schools and districts have a supportive environment, selecting interventions grounded in research, and applying effective strategies for implementation, educational leaders can drive meaningful change that improves student outcomes. Together, these three buckets provide a comprehensive framework for bridging the gap between research and practice. In the chapters following, we will dive deeper and provide tools and resources to work through each "bucket."

Bibliography

Damschroder, L. J., Aron, D. C., Keith, R. E., Kirsh, S. R., Alexander, J. A., & Lowery, J. C. (2009). Fostering implementation of health services research findings into practice: A consolidated framework for advancing implementation science. *Implementation Science, 4*(1), 50.

Fixsen, D. L., & Blase, K. A. (2020). Active implementation frameworks. In P. Nilsen & S. A. Birken (Eds.), *Handbook on Implementation Science* (pp. 62–68). Edward Elgar Publishing.

CHAPTER THREE

Understanding Implementation Science

The field of education is continuously evolving, with new research and evidence-based practices emerging regularly. However, one of the persistent challenges has been ensuring that these evidence-based practices are effectively adopted, implemented, and sustained in real-world educational settings. This is where the field of Implementation Science becomes invaluable. By focusing on the systematic study of how to design, assess, and promote the adoption of evidence-based practices, Implementation Science provides the tools to bridge the gap between research and classroom practice. This chapter will explore the key concepts of Implementation Science, its importance in education, and the processes involved in ensuring that educational innovations make a lasting impact.

In the context of education, Implementation Science focuses on integrating research-based educational interventions, programs, and strategies into schools, ensuring that these innovations are adopted and maintained over time.

Implementation Science is grounded in the idea that three critical component parts, when multiplied together, equate to the intended outcomes. Think of it like a simple mathematical equation where 1 x 1 x 1 = 1. If any of the component parts is zero (in this equation, a component part not being addressed would be zero), then the result is also always going to be zero.

1	x	1	x	1	=	1

Each of the component parts is of equal value, let's say one whole, and without any of the component parts, the result is nothing.

1	x	0	x	1	=	0

Figure 3.1. Equation

Fixsen, D. L., Blase, K. A., Duda, M. A., Naoom, S. F., & Van Dyke, M. (2010). Implementation of evidence-based treatments for children and adolescents: Research findings and their implications for the future. *Psychiatric Clinics of North America, 33*(2), 223–240.

1. To achieve the intended result, addressing each of the component parts fully, like a whole number, and not partially, like a fraction, is required to achieve the desired outcome and
2. Each of the component parts is held together as an equation through a common "function" (multiplication). Without the mathematical function, the component parts are simply isolated whole numbers.

Planning for and Selecting the Curriculum *Have you selected the right HQMI?*	x	Developing & Implementing the Roadmap *Are you on a path to success by implementing, monitoring, assessing and making changes as needed?*	x	Creating the Context and the Conditions *Are you ready?*	=	Intended Outcome

Figure 3.2. Equation Parts

Carlson, J., & Neil, C. (2024). Tying it all together [Image]. Imagine Learning.

Once we understand that achieving our intended results requires both fully addressing the component parts and identifying a common function that inextricably links them together, we can see how Implementation Science gives us the foundation needed to finally realize the essential goal of any educational institution—positive and equitable outcomes for all students.

Effective Planning and Selection of Curriculum

Implementation Science also emphasizes the importance of strategic planning. Schools and districts must carefully plan for each implementation stage, considering the specific needs of their context and the challenges they may face. Strategic planning involves setting clear goals, developing a timeline, identifying necessary resources, and engaging stakeholders.

Effective planning ensures that schools are prepared to implement the intervention with fidelity and have the support systems to sustain it over time. It is essential to the selection of high-quality instructional curricula and materials, a critical component of school and district reform. Implementation Science provides a structured framework that ensures selections are research-based, contextually relevant, and set up for effective implementation. In this strategic context, choosing instructional materials is not a single event but part of an extensive system that prioritizes alignment with student needs, teacher capacity, and organizational goals. Strategic planning involves not only selecting an evidence-based curriculum but also establishing a timeline for rollout, preparing for professional development, and building structures to support classroom integration and fidelity in application. This multi-phase approach ensures that chosen materials are consistently used to meet instructional goals, with an ongoing system for evaluating and refining effectiveness based on classroom outcomes and teacher feedback (Fixsen et al., 2005). By embedding these steps into a cohesive plan, districts can create a sustainable plan to reach their intended outcomes.

The selection of high-quality instructional curricula and materials is a critical component of school and district reform efforts, and Implementation Science provides a structured framework for ensuring that these selections are both research based and effectively implemented. In the context of Implementation Science, choosing instructional materials is not a one-time decision but part of a more extensive system that ensures alignment with student needs, teacher capacity, and organizational goals.

A high-quality curriculum must be grounded in evidence, meaning it should be supported by rigorous research demonstrating its effectiveness in improving student outcomes. Implementation Science stresses the importance of selecting materials tested through randomized control trials or other reliable methods, ensuring they are effective across diverse populations and contexts (Hedges & Rhoads, 2010). When districts select curricula based on sound research, they lay the groundwork for more effective instruction, reducing the trial-and-error process that can otherwise lead to inconsistent student performance.

While the research base is critical, implementation science also highlights the importance of selecting curricula that align with local contexts, including student demographics, teacher capacity, and available resources. A curriculum that works well in one district may not have the same impact in another if there are significant differences in student needs or teacher preparedness (Century & Cassata, 2016). Therefore, districts must consider how well a curriculum fits their specific context. For instance, selecting materials that support English Language Learners (ELLs) or students with learning disabilities can ensure broader applicability and effectiveness across diverse classrooms. This alignment process is backed by needs assessments and stakeholder input, ensuring that the curriculum meets the practical realities of the schools where it will be implemented.

Effective Implementation

Effective implementation refers to the processes and strategies that ensure the intervention is delivered as intended and achieves its desired outcomes. This bucket encompasses the mechanisms, such as training, coaching, monitoring, and problem-solving, that facilitate the successful application of the intervention in real-world settings.

"Effective implementation involves ensuring that evidence-based practices are implemented with fidelity and supported by ongoing training, coaching, and performance feedback" (Fixsen et al., 2005, p. 27). One added layer from this author is integrity. Oftentimes, fidelity is a checklist of actions to be noted, while integrity aligns with the pedagogy and practice. Even a well-designed intervention in a supportive context can fail to produce meaningful outcomes without effective implementation.

Consider a school district that has adopted a new science curriculum. For effective implementation, teachers must be trained to use the curriculum, receive ongoing coaching to refine their practices, and be provided with opportunities for feedback and reflection. Additionally, the district might establish monitoring systems to track progress and make necessary adjustments. Effective implementation ensures that the curriculum is adopted and used in a way that leads to improved student outcomes.

"The core of Implementation Science is the application of evidence-based practices, which have a solid foundation of research demonstrating their effectiveness" (Fixsen et al., 2005, p. 19). An effective intervention has been rigorously tested and proven to produce positive results when applied correctly. However, it is equally important to ensure that the chosen intervention aligns with the goals and context of the implementing organization.

For instance, a district may choose a behavior management program that has been shown to reduce disciplinary incidents in urban school settings. The intervention has demonstrated effectiveness in multiple trials and is considered evidence-based. To be effective, however, the district must ensure that the program is implemented with fidelity and that teachers receive appropriate training and resources to deliver the program as designed.

Encompassing all stages of the implementation process include:

1. **Exploration:** Identifying the needs and determining which evidence-based interventions would best address these needs.
2. **Installation:** Preparing for the intervention's adoption, which might include securing resources, training staff, and setting up necessary infrastructure.
3. **Initial Implementation:** Introducing the intervention into practice, often accompanied by monitoring and adjustments based on initial feedback.
4. **Full Implementation:** The intervention becomes fully integrated into regular practice, with continued monitoring to ensure fidelity.
5. **Sustainability:** Ensuring the long-term maintenance of the intervention and its continued effectiveness.

Each of these stages requires careful planning, resources, and commitment to ensure the successful adoption of evidence-based practices.

Enabling Context

Enabling context refers to the organizational, cultural, and environmental conditions that support an intervention's successful adoption and sustainability. This context includes factors such as leadership, infrastructure, policy alignment, and stakeholder buy-in, all of which create a conducive environment for change.

"Implementation efforts are more likely to succeed when the organizational context is supportive, with strong leadership, sufficient resources, and an organizational culture that embraces change" (Aarons et al., 2011). Enabling context ensures that schools and districts are prepared for the complexities of implementation and have the infrastructure and support systems necessary to foster success.

For example, a school district implementing a new literacy intervention must ensure its context is ready for change. This might involve securing support from district leaders, aligning the intervention with existing policies, providing necessary resources (e.g., training materials and technology), and fostering a culture that values evidence-based practices. Even the most effective intervention will struggle to take hold without these elements.

Bridging the Research-Practice Gap

One of Implementation Science's key contributions is its role in bridging the research-***to***-practice gap. There is often a disconnect between what research shows to be effective and what is actually practiced in classrooms. This gap can be attributed to a variety of factors, including a lack of resources, insufficient training, or resistance to change.

Implementation Science provides a framework for overcoming these barriers, helping educators and policymakers move beyond the question of "what works" to "what works in practice" and "how to make it work here." This shift is critical because it acknowledges that successful implementation requires not only evidence of effectiveness but also attention to context, culture, and other local factors.

By focusing on the practical aspects of implementation, this field helps ensure that evidence-based practices are adapted to fit the specific needs of individual schools and districts, ultimately leading to better outcomes for students.

Improving Educational Outcomes

The ultimate goal of Implementation Science in education is to improve student outcomes by ensuring that effective practices are implemented and sustained over time. Whether it is a new reading program, a behavioral intervention, or a technology initiative, the success of any educational innovation depends on how well it is implemented.

Research has shown that even the most effective interventions can fail to produce positive outcomes if not implemented with fidelity. This is where Implementation Science plays a critical role—it provides the tools and strategies to ensure that interventions are delivered as intended and that any barriers to implementation are addressed.

By applying the principles of Implementation Science, schools can create the conditions necessary for educational innovations to succeed. This involves engaging stakeholders, providing ongoing training and support, and continuously monitoring progress to ensure effective intervention.

Key Concepts in Implementation Science

Stages of Implementation

As noted earlier, Implementation Science typically involves several stages, each critical to the process's success. The stages include exploration, installation, initial implementation, full implementation, and sustainability. Each stage requires different strategies and resources, and the success of each stage builds on the previous one.

For example, during the exploration phase, schools may conduct needs assessments and identify evidence-based practices that align with their goals. During installation, they may focus on securing the necessary resources and training staff. During initial implementation, they may pilot the intervention and adjust based on feedback. Finally, during full implementation and sustainability, they work to integrate the intervention into everyday practice and ensure that it continues to produce positive outcomes over time.

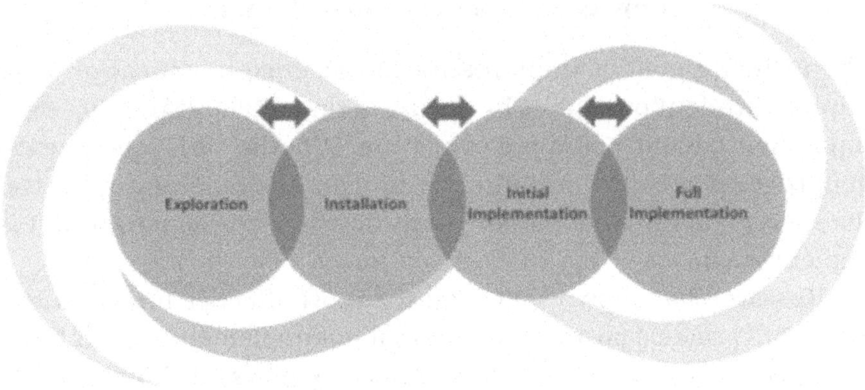

Figure 3.3. Stages of Implementation

Fixsen, D. L., & Blase, K. A. (2020). Active implementation frameworks. In P. Nilsen & S. A. Birken (Eds.), *Handbook on implementation science* (pp. 62–68). Edward Elgar Publishing.

Key Drivers of Implementation

In addition to the stages of implementation, Implementation Science also emphasizes the importance of key drivers that support successful implementation. These drivers include:

- **Competency Drivers**: Ensuring that staff have the necessary knowledge, skills, and competencies to implement the intervention effectively. This may involve professional development, coaching, and ongoing support.
- **Organization Drivers:** Creating the organizational infrastructure necessary to support implementation, including adequate resources, leadership, and data systems.
- **Leadership Drivers:** Strong leadership is essential for guiding the implementation process, addressing challenges, and creating a culture of continuous improvement.

These drivers work together to create the conditions necessary for successful implementation.

Conclusion

Implementation Science provides a comprehensive framework for ensuring that evidence-based practices are effectively adopted, implemented, and sustained in real-world settings. By understanding and applying the principles of Implementation Science, school districts can bridge the gap between research and practice, ultimately improving educational outcomes for all students. Through stages of implementation, key drivers, and strategic planning, districts can foster an environment where innovations thrive and make a lasting impact.

Implementation Science will remain essential as education evolves in guiding schools and districts toward successful and sustainable change. By focusing on the practical aspects of implementation, this field helps ensure that effective practices are adopted and maintained over time, leading to long-term improvements in student outcomes.

Questions for Reflection

To deepen your understanding of Implementation Science and its application in education, consider the following questions:

1. What are the key stages of Implementation Science, and why is it important to systematically move through them?
2. How does Implementation Science help bridge the gap between educational research and classroom practice?
3. What are some of the critical drivers of successful implementation, and how can schools ensure these drivers are in place?
4. How can strategic planning help schools and districts overcome the challenges of implementing evidence-based practices?
5. What role does leadership play in the successful implementation and sustainability of educational interventions?

Bibliography

Aarons, G. A., Hurlburt, M., & Horwitz, S. M. (2011). Advancing a conceptual model of evidence-based practice implementation in public service sectors. *Administration and Policy in Mental Health and Mental Health Services Research, 38*(1), 4–23.

Century, J., & Cassata, A. (2016a). Implementation research: Finding common ground on what, how, why, where, and who. *Review of Research in Education, 40*(1), 169–215.

Century, J., & Cassata, A. (2016b). Conceptual foundations for measuring the implementation of educational innovations. *Journal of Educational Research, 109*(1), 1–19.

Fixsen, D. L., Blase, K. A., Metz, A., & Van Dyke, M. K. (2013). Statewide implementation of evidence-based programs. *Exceptional Children, 79*(2), 213–230. https://doi.org/10.1177/001440291307900206

Fixsen, D. L., Blase, K. A., Metz, A., & Van Dyke, M. (2015). Implementation science. In R. Joshi & S. Paciorek (Eds.), *The future of evidence-based education* (pp. 14–25). Harvard Education Press.

Fixsen, D. L., Naoom, S. F., Blase, K. A., Friedman, R. M., & Wallace, F. (2005). *Implementation research: A synthesis of the literature*. University of South Florida, Louis de la Parte Florida Mental Health Institute, National Implementation Research Network. https://nirn.fpg.unc.edu/resources/implementation-research-synthesis-literature

Hedges, L. V., & Rhoads, C. (2010). Statistical power analysis in education research. *Journal of Educational and Behavioral Statistics, 35*(1), 2–24.

CHAPTER FOUR

Tenets of Implementation Science

Implementation Science is a field dedicated to effectively understanding how to bring evidence-based interventions into practice. It goes beyond the research of what works to focus on how to make these interventions work in specific contexts. The success of implementing new initiatives in education hinges on applying fundamental principles of Implementation Science. This chapter explores three critical tenets of Implementation Science—evidence-based practices, contextual fit, and stakeholder engagement—each of which plays an essential role in ensuring that interventions have a lasting and positive impact in schools and districts.

Evidence-Based Practices: Focus on Proven Interventions

One of the core principles of Implementation Science is the emphasis on using evidence-based practices—interventions and strategies that have been rigorously tested and proven effective in improving outcomes. Evidence-based practices are supported by a robust body of research that demonstrates their efficacy across multiple settings. This focus ensures that schools are implementing strategies that are highly likely to succeed, rather than relying on unproven or anecdotal methods.

"The core of Implementation Science is the application of evidence-based practices, which have a solid foundation of research demonstrating their effectiveness" (Fixsen et al., 2005, p. 19). The emphasis on evidence-based practices helps to maximize the likelihood that the interventions will produce meaningful improvements in student outcomes. It also provides educators and policymakers with confidence that their efforts are backed by solid research.

However, merely selecting an evidence-based practice is not sufficient for successful implementation. The chosen intervention must be implemented with fidelity—meaning it must be applied consistently and as intended in the research studies that demonstrated its effectiveness. Even the most well-researched intervention can fail to produce the desired results without integrity and fidelity.

The Importance of Integrity

Integrity refers to adherence to ethical principles, honesty, and transparency while adopting and integrating evidence-based practices. While fidelity ensures that an intervention is implemented as designed, integrity ensures that the entire process is carried out with ethical responsibility and respect for all stakeholders involved. Maintaining integrity is crucial to sustaining trust and credibility for long-term success in any school or district initiative.

Upholding integrity means committing to fairness, openness, and a genuine focus on the well-being of both students and staff. Schools often face challenges such as limited resources, diverse student populations, or stakeholder resistance when implementing new interventions. In these cases, ensuring that actions are aligned with ethical standards becomes even more critical. Decision-makers must navigate these difficulties without compromising the core values of transparency and accountability. Much like fidelity, integrity is a guiding principle that ensures schools remain committed to doing what is right, even when the path to successful implementation is complex.

Implementation Science emphasizes the importance of ethical decision-making throughout the process. Just as schools use monitoring tools to assess fidelity, they must also apply measures to consistently address ethical considerations. This involves transparency in communication, openness to feedback, and the willingness to hold all participants accountable for their roles in the implementation process. By incorporating frameworks that promote ethical integrity, schools can navigate challenging situations without sacrificing trust or the quality of their intervention.

To ensure integrity is upheld, schools should establish regular ethical reviews, seek stakeholder input, and engage in reflective practices. These strategies allow for continuous self-assessment and ensure that decisions made during implementation align with the institution's overall mission and values. Furthermore, ongoing dialogue around ethical issues helps educators and staff navigate the complexities of implementation, fostering an environment where integrity is prioritized at every level.

The emphasis on integrity has been a driving force in reshaping the understanding and implementation of structured literacy, particularly in addressing diverse learners' needs. The renewed focus on integrity within this framework has led educators and policymakers to reconsider the ethical implications of reading instruction, particularly for students who have been underserved by less effective methods such as balanced literacy. Maintaining integrity in structured literacy involves a commitment to transparency, fidelity to the research, and a focus on equity, ensuring that every student receives high-quality, scientifically sound instruction.

One area where integrity has transformed the understanding of structured literacy is in addressing the long-standing achievement gaps for students with dyslexia and other reading difficulties. For decades, many educational systems relied on instructional methods that were not aligned with the science of reading, resulting in poor outcomes for students who struggled with decoding and other foundational skills (Shanahan, 2020). By upholding integrity, schools and districts have begun implementing structured literacy practices with fidelity, ensuring that students receive the explicit instruction they need to become proficient readers.

By adhering to the principles of integrity, educators are bound to follow evidence-based practices and remain transparent and accountable to their students, families, and communities. This approach has helped educators move away from approaches that lacked empirical support, such as whole language and balanced literacy, which often failed to meet the needs of struggling readers (Hanford, 2022). The ethical mandate to "do no harm" has underscored the importance of providing all students, especially those with learning disabilities, access to structured literacy, which research has consistently shown to be more effective for teaching foundational reading skills (Kilpatrick, 2015).

As schools adopt structured literacy, integrity has led to more inclusive instructional practices that honor the diverse needs of learners. Educators have contributed to a growing national movement that prioritizes the literacy success of all students by focusing on evidence-based strategies and holding themselves accountable to delivering high-quality instruction. This ethical commitment has helped close achievement gaps, fostered greater educational equity, and provided a clearer path forward for educators striving to implement reading instruction that is both effective and just.

The Importance of Fidelity

Fidelity refers to the degree to which an intervention is delivered as intended. When implementing evidence-based practices, it is essential to maintain fidelity to the core components of the intervention while also considering necessary adaptations for the local context. Schools must balance adhering to the intervention's evidence-based design and adjusting to their unique environments.

Fidelity in implementing a new curriculum is often reduced to a procedural task of "checking off a list," where educators focus more on completing specific actions rather than ensuring the quality and depth of the implementation process. This approach can lead to superficial compliance, where schools meet technical requirements without fully engaging with the core principles or goals of the curriculum (Fixsen et al., 2015). While fidelity tools such as checklists can help ensure that key components of the curriculum are in place, they often fail to capture whether the curriculum is being delivered with the intended rigor or effectiveness (Durlak & DuPre, 2008). For example, research on evidence-based reading instruction shows that simply following the steps outlined in a curriculum does not guarantee successful outcomes if teachers are not also given the training and support needed to adapt these materials thoughtfully to their classroom contexts (Desimone & Garet, 2015).

Implementation Science provides tools and strategies to help educators monitor fidelity throughout the implementation process.

This often involves regular assessments, coaching, and ongoing professional development to ensure that teachers and staff consistently apply the intervention as designed.

Adaptation to Local Contexts

While evidence-based practices are essential, their effectiveness often depends on how well they fit the specific context in which they are being implemented. Schools and districts differ widely in student populations, organizational structures, cultural norms, and available resources. Therefore, adapting interventions to fit the local context is critical while maintaining the core components that make the practice effective. No two schools/districts are the same which makes the framework especially powerful.

"Interventions must be tailored to the local context to be effective, addressing unique needs and challenges" (Damschroder et al., 2009). This adaptation process ensures that the intervention remains relevant and responsive to the unique needs of the community it serves. It also increases the likelihood that the intervention will be accepted and sustained over time.

Balancing Integrity, Fidelity, and Adaptation

A key challenge in Implementation Science is balancing the need for integrity and fidelity with the need for contextual adaptation. While integrity and fidelity ensure that the core elements of the evidence-based practice are preserved, adaptation ensures that the intervention is feasible and relevant within the local context. Successful implementation requires careful consideration of all factors, with an understanding that some adjustments may be necessary to account for local conditions without compromising the integrity of the intervention.

Involving Key Stakeholders

Engaging stakeholders is a fundamental tenet of Implementation Science. Stakeholders include anyone interested in the intervention's success, such as teachers, administrators, parents, students, and community members. Their involvement is crucial because the intervention will most directly impact these individuals and is essential to its success.

"Active involvement of stakeholders throughout the implementation process enhances buy-in and ensures the relevance of the intervention" (Moullin et al., 2020, p. 4). Stakeholders provide valuable insights into the local context, offer feedback on how the intervention is being received, and help to identify potential barriers to successful implementation. By involving stakeholders early and often, educators can build the buy-in necessary for sustained change.

Addressing Resistance to Change

One of the challenges of stakeholder engagement is managing resistance to change. Even when an intervention is supported by strong evidence and fits the local context, individuals may be hesitant to adopt new practices. Resistance can stem from various factors, including fear of the unknown, lack of confidence in the new approach, or attachment to existing methods.

Implementation Science provides strategies for addressing resistance by emphasizing the importance of open communication, professional development, and ongoing support. By involving stakeholders in the planning and implementation process, schools can identify potential sources of resistance early and address them proactively. This might include providing additional training, offering reassurances about the benefits of the intervention, or creating opportunities for individuals to see the new practices in action before fully committing.

Conclusion

The tenets of Implementation Science—evidence-based practices, contextual fit, and stakeholder engagement—provide a comprehensive framework for effectively implementing new educational interventions. Schools can maximize the chances of successful implementation and sustainability by focusing on proven interventions, adapting them to the local context, and actively involving stakeholders throughout the process. These principles ensure that educational innovations are adopted and tailored to meet the community's unique needs, leading to better student outcomes and long-term improvements in academic practice.

As schools and districts continue to adopt new programs and practices, the principles of Implementation Science offer a pathway to ensuring their success. By emphasizing fidelity, contextual fit, and stakeholder engagement, Implementation Science helps bridge the gap between research and practice, making it possible for schools to implement evidence-based interventions in effective and sustainable ways.

Questions for Reflection

To deepen your understanding of the tenets of Implementation Science and their application in education, consider the following questions:

1. Why is it important to focus on evidence-based practices when implementing new educational interventions?
2. How can schools balance the need for fidelity with adaptation to the local context?
3. What role does stakeholder engagement play in the success of an implementation effort, and how can schools effectively involve stakeholders throughout the process?
4. What strategies can schools use to address resistance to change when implementing new evidence-based practices?
5. How can contextual fit and stakeholder engagement help ensure that educational interventions are adopted and sustained over time?

Bibliography

Damschroder, L. J., Aron, D. C., Keith, R. E., Kirsh, S. R., Alexander, J. A., & Lowery, J. C. (2009). Fostering implementation of health services research findings into practice: A consolidated framework for advancing implementation science. *Implementation Science, 4*(1), 50.

Desimone, L. M., & Garet, M. S. (2015). Best practices in teachers' professional development in the United States. *Psychology, Society & Education, 7*(3), 252–263.

Durlak, J. A., & DuPre, E. P. (2008). Implementation matters: A review of research on the influence of implementation on program outcomes and the factors affecting implementation. *American Journal of Community Psychology, 41*(3), 327–350.

Fixsen, D., Blase, K., Metz, A., & Van Dyke, M. (2015). Implementation science. In R. Joshi & S. Paciorek (Eds.), *The future of evidence-based education* (pp. 14–25). Harvard Education Press.

Fixsen, D. L., Blase, K. A., Naoom, S. F., & Wallace, F. (2005). Core implementation components. *Research on Social Work Practice, 15*(5), 531–539.

Hanford, E. (2022, October 20). *Sold a story: How teaching kids to read went so wrong*. APM Reports. https://www.apmreports.org/episode/2022/10/20/sold-a-story

Kilpatrick, D. A. (2015). *Essentials of assessing, preventing, and overcoming reading difficulties*. Wiley.

Moullin, J. C., Sabater-Hernández, D., Fernandez-Llimos, F., & Benrimoj, S. I. (2020). A consolidated framework for implementation science. *Research in Social and Administrative Pharmacy, 16*(4), 528–543.

Shanahan, T. (2020). What constitutes evidence-based literacy instruction? *Reading Research Quarterly, 55*(S1), S361–S372.

PART III

Enabling Context

Implementation Science is a vital field in education, focusing on the effective integration of evidence-based practices into educational settings. One of the critical components of this science is the enabling context, which plays a significant role in determining whether innovations are successfully adopted, sustained, and scaled within schools. An enabling context involves understanding and optimizing the specific conditions, resources, and cultural factors that support or hinder implementation efforts. Without a supportive context, even the most well-designed and evidence-backed interventions may struggle to take root and thrive.

1	x	1	x	1	=	1

Each of the component parts is of equal value, let's say one whole, and without any of the component parts, the result is nothing.

1	x	0	x	1	=	0

Figure III.1. Equation

Fixsen, D. L., Blase, K. A., Duda, M. A., Naoom, S. F., & Van Dyke, M. (2010). Implementation of evidence-based treatments for children and adolescents: Research findings and their implications for the future. *Psychiatric Clinics of North America, 33*(2), 223–240.

As the formula above shows, enabling context is part of an equation to reach intended outcomes. We have put this chapter before Effective Practice and Effective Implementation for this playbook due to the planning process and teaming generally required. We will explore the concept of enabling context, its significance in the implementation process, and the factors that influence it in educational settings. By recognizing and addressing these factors, educators and school leaders can create an environment conducive to long-term, meaningful change.

Defining Enabling Context

The enabling context refers to the environmental, organizational, and cultural conditions that facilitate or hinder the implementation of educational innovations. It includes a range of factors such as leadership, staff readiness, school culture, community involvement, resources, policies, and socioeconomic conditions. Understanding these contextual elements is critical for tailoring interventions to fit the specific needs and circumstances of a school or district.

"Implementation science in education requires an intricate understanding of the local context, which includes factors such as school culture, administrative support, and socio-economic conditions" (Fixsen et al., 2015). The enabling context is not static; it is dynamic and multidimensional, continuously evolving as new challenges and opportunities arise. As such, educators must remain adaptable and responsive to changes in the context to ensure sustained success.

The Multidimensional Nature of Enabling Context

School Culture

School culture plays a foundational role in shaping the enabling context. School culture encompasses the values, beliefs, norms, and practices that define how educators, students, and staff interact within a school. A positive, collaborative, and innovation-friendly culture can support the implementation of new educational practices by fostering openness to change and encouraging experimentation. Conversely, a resistant or fragmented school culture can create barriers to implementation, as staff may be less willing to adopt new practices or may struggle to work cohesively toward shared goals.

A case study of a middle school in Seattle highlights the importance of school culture in enabling context. When the school attempted to implement a new STEM curriculum, initial efforts were met with resistance due to a culture of skepticism toward new initiatives. Recognizing this, the school's leadership team shifted their approach, focusing on building trust through professional development and creating opportunities for teacher collaboration. Over time, the school culture became more supportive of innovation, enabling the successful integration of the STEM program.

Administrative Support

Strong administrative support is another critical factor in creating an enabling context. School and district leaders play a pivotal role in providing the vision, resources, and accountability necessary for successful implementation. Leadership that is engaged, responsive, and committed to the innovation can help overcome challenges by offering guidance, securing resources, and fostering an environment of collaboration.

According to research, "the success of any educational innovation is heavily influenced by the environment in which it is implemented" (Century & Cassata, 2016, pp. 171–172). For instance, in a district in Texas implementing a literacy intervention, strong administrative support was a key enabler. The superintendent and school principals actively promoted the program, allocated necessary resources, and regularly communicated with staff to reinforce the importance of the initiative. This high level of administrative support created a conducive environment for successful implementation.

Resources and Infrastructure

Adequate resources and infrastructure are also essential elements of an enabling context. This includes material resources such as funding, technology, instructional materials, and facilities, as well as human resources, such as skilled teachers, coaches, and support staff. Schools and districts with sufficient resources are better equipped to implement and sustain new practices effectively.

For example, a school district in Colorado attempted to implement a blended learning initiative but faced significant challenges due to limited technological infrastructure and inadequate training for teachers. Despite having a well-researched and promising intervention, the lack of resources created a significant barrier to success. Only after the district secured additional funding for technology upgrades and provided extensive professional development for teachers did the initiative begin to gain traction.

Socioeconomic Conditions

Socioeconomic conditions within the school community also play a crucial role in shaping the enabling context. Schools located in low-income areas may face unique challenges, such as limited funding, higher student needs, and external stressors affecting student engagement and teacher capacity. However, these challenges can be addressed with tailored interventions that account for these contextual realities.

For example, a Title I elementary school in New York faced numerous barriers to implementing a social-emotional learning (SEL) program, including high rates of student absenteeism and a lack of parental involvement. However, the school leadership recognized the socioeconomic conditions of the community and adapted the program by incorporating after-school activities and parent engagement workshops. This approach helped address the community's specific needs and allowed the SEL program to flourish.

The Role of Adaptability in Enabling Context

Adaptability is a key characteristic of an enabling context given the dynamic nature of school environments. School leaders and educators must be flexible and responsive to changes in the local context, whether these changes involve shifts in policy, budget constraints, or emerging needs among students and staff. Adaptability involves continuously assessing the context and adjusting the implementation plan as needed to ensure the intervention remains viable and effective.

"An enabling context is not a fixed entity; it is continually shaped by the interactions between the intervention and the local environment" (Damschroder et al., 2009, p. 5). Schools that prioritize adaptability are more likely to achieve long-term success with their interventions because they can adjust to unforeseen challenges and leverage new opportunities to enhance their implementation efforts.

Conclusion

The enabling context is a critical component of Implementation Science in education. By recognizing the multidimensional and dynamic nature of school environments—encompassing factors such as school culture, administrative support, resources, and socioeconomic conditions—educators and leaders can create the conditions necessary for the successful and sustainable implementation of evidence-based practices. Understanding and optimizing this context allows schools and districts to bridge the gap between research and practice, ultimately leading to better student educational outcomes.

As schools and districts continue to adopt innovations, the enabling context will remain a central focus in ensuring that these initiatives are adopted and thrive in the long term. Educators can foster environments where research-backed practices lead to meaningful and lasting change by continuously assessing and adapting the enabling context.

Questions for Reflection

To deepen your understanding of the enabling context in Implementation Science and its application in educational settings, consider the following questions:

1. What are the key elements of an enabling context that influence the success of educational innovations?
2. How can school leaders and educators assess and improve the enabling context to support the implementation of evidence-based practices?
3. What role does school culture play in shaping the enabling context, and how can schools cultivate a culture that supports innovation?
4. How can schools in low-resource settings address the challenges posed by limited infrastructure and socioeconomic conditions to create a more supportive enabling context?
5. Why is adaptability important in maintaining a conducive enabling context, and what strategies can schools use to remain flexible in response to changes?

Bibliography

Century, J., & Cassata, A. (2016). Implementation research: finding common ground on what, how, why, where, and who. *Review of Research in Education, 40*, 169–215. https://doi.org/10.3102/0091732X16665332.

Damschroder, L. J., Aron, D. C., Keith, R. E., Kirsh, S. R., Alexander, J. A., & Lowery, J. C. (2009). Fostering implementation of health services research findings into practice: A consolidated framework for advancing implementation science. *Implementation Science, 4*(1), 50.

Fixsen, D. L., Blase, K. A., Metz, A., & Van Dyke, M. (2015). Implementation science. In R. Joshi & S. Paciorek (Eds.), *The future of evidence-based education* (pp. 14–25). Harvard Education Press.

CHAPTER FIVE

Building Teams

Forming and sustaining effective curriculum review teams are central to this process. These teams foster stakeholder collaboration, harness diverse perspectives, and empower educators and community members to drive meaningful change. This chapter explores how districts can build and sustain effective curriculum review teams, emphasizing collaboration, diversity, and structured processes.

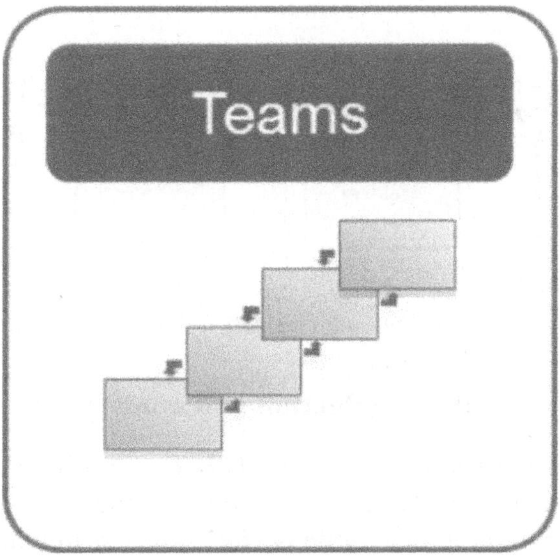

Figure 5.1. Teams

Fixsen, D. L., & Blase, K. A. (2020). Active implementation frameworks. In P. Nilsen & S. A. Birken (Eds.), *Handbook on implementation science* (pp. 62–68). Edward Elgar Publishing.

The Needs Assessment

A needs assessment is a systematic process used to identify the gaps between the current conditions in your school system and the desired outcomes. It involves gathering data and feedback from various stakeholders—students, teachers, parents, and the community—to understand what is working well and where improvements are needed. The needs assessment process allows the Implementation Team to deeply understand the current conditions, hypothesize root causes, validate problems, and then prioritize and set goals to develop a thoughtful action plan.

The needs assessment helps your Implementation Team ensure:

- That the data being collected and analyzed are valid and free of bias
- That the underlying root causes become the focus
- That the goals being set are the "right ones"

Needs Assessment Process

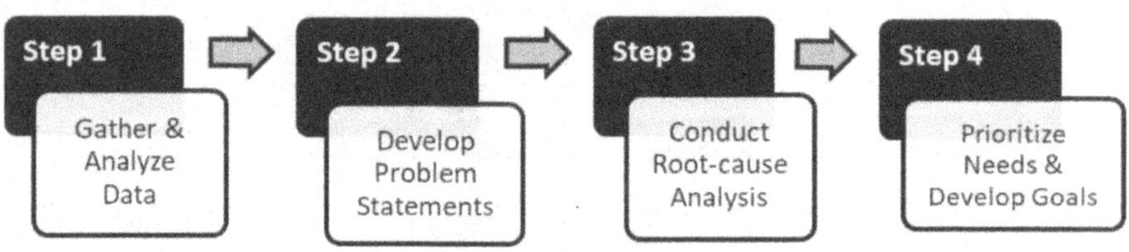

Figure 5.2. Needs Assessment

Carlson, J. (2020). *Needs Assessment Process* [Figure]. Fall River Public Schools.

Data Collection and Analysis

The data needed should have already been identified and collected as detailed earlier in this process. This includes, but is not limited to, gathering data on academic performance, attendance, behavior reports, programmatic results, teacher feedback, student surveys, and community input. Your Implementation Team can only rely on the data collected to build their needs assessment; therefore it is essential that you have good data collection. Remember your Implementation Team cannot limit themselves by only taking a "balcony view" of the data; they must be able to look at multiple data points at the district, school site, and classroom level to conduct an authentic needs assessment.

Ask:

- Does the data we have collected provide information at the district, building/school site, and classroom level?
- What data points are we asking for from teachers, what standardized data from the school, what state indicators at the district level?
- Are we using a data dashboard that can drill down from district level to school site, to classrooms?

What approaches can we use to understand the story the data are telling us?

When it comes to analyzing data, it is true that data are just data, but the analysis process is a human process, and influence and bias can skew our interpretations and findings. Therefore taking the time to minimize bias in data analysis is essential to ensure that decisions and actions taken in your school systems are fair, equitable, and truly effective. Implementation Teams need to engage in data analysis approaches that help minimize implicit and explicit biases.

Avoid relying on a single data point (e.g., standardized test scores). Instead, incorporate a variety of data types such as formative assessments, student surveys, attendance records, teacher observations, and qualitative feedback. By triangulating data, biases inherent in one data source can be mitigated by using others. Break down the data by various subgroups (race, gender, socioeconomic status, disability, etc.) to uncover disparities that may be hidden in aggregate data to prevent biases related to overlooking specific groups or assuming that overall trends apply equally to all students. Ensure that data are gathered from a wide range of sources, including students from different backgrounds, learning abilities, and socioeconomic statuses, as well as teachers, parents, and the community. This reduces selection bias, where certain groups might be underrepresented, leading to skewed conclusions.

Anonymize or "blind" the data during the analysis phase, so that decisions are made without knowing specific details (e.g., student names, genders, or socioeconomic backgrounds) that could introduce unconscious bias. This reduces confirmation bias, where people might unintentionally favor data that aligns with preconceived notions or expectations.

Define clear and objective criteria for data interpretation before starting the analysis. For example, use rubrics for evaluating student performance or teaching effectiveness. Predefined criteria help to prevent subjective interpretation of data based on personal biases or assumptions.

Engage multiple team members in reviewing the data and findings. Different perspectives can help identify potential biases in interpretation or methodology. Collaboration encourages diverse viewpoints and can help identify blind spots or biases that an individual might miss. Consider engaging external experts or use external audits to review your data collection, analysis processes, and conclusions. Outside perspectives can provide a fresh look at your data practices and may uncover biases or gaps that internal teams might overlook.

Provide ongoing training for your team on implicit bias and how it can affect data interpretation, decision-making, and interactions with students. Awareness of bias helps individuals be more reflective and cautious when analyzing data, reducing the influence of unconscious bias.

Ask:

- Is our data labeled with nonidentifiable markers like "Site A," "Classroom B," etc.?
- Have we engaged in collaborative processes using systematic approaches to identify gaps and understand root causes?
- Are we engaging in personal growth and development to address our unconscious biases?

Analyzing Data

The purpose of reviewing all of the data is to try and understand the story that the data are telling. Your Implementation Team is looking for trends and metrics that give an understanding of what's happening within the district, at school sites, and at the classroom level.

By understanding the current conditions, the Implementation Team can better understand the "facts" of what's working and what's not working. The findings are the foundations of articulating the problems to be addressed. And your team can feel confident that their findings are supported by data, not opinions, influence, or bias. Your data review provides the Implementation Team with a clear, data-informed understanding of the district's current conditions.

ASK:

- Did we review the data and identify recurring patterns or trends?
- Have we used historical data to identify concerning trends over time?
- Are we defining the gap between current performance and the desired goal?
- Have we compared the actual data results with benchmarks or goals, quantified the difference (performance gap), and described its impact?
- Have we identified the stakeholders most affected by the problem and used data to describe the magnitude of the impact on each group?
- Are we noting broader systemic or structural issues revealed by the data?
- Are we analyzing the data for evidence of institutional or systemic barriers?

Problems and Root Causes

As the Educational Leader of the Implementation Team, once you have completed your data review, the next step is to articulate findings as "problem statements." To do this well, there is value in framing the problem in the underlying cause rather than surface-level symptoms.

ASK:

- Are we being concise and specific and avoiding overly broad or vague language?

- Are we using measurable data and quantifying the problem whenever possible?
- Are we emphasizing how the problem affects key outcomes (student achievement, engagement, equity)?
- Are we ensuring the problem is within the scope of what the team can address?
- Are we tying the problem to our values and goals (e.g., equity, inclusion, academic excellence)?

Prioritization and Action Planning:

Based on the gaps identified, the school or district must do the work of prioritizing the most critical areas for improvement. Action planning strategies are developed to address the identified needs, often tied to professional development, resource allocation, curriculum adjustments, or policy changes. Needs assessments provide concrete data to guide leadership decisions. Rather than relying on assumptions, educators can focus resources on areas that will have the most significant impact on student outcomes. It helps schools provide targeted interventions, ensuring that all students, especially those at risk, receive the necessary support. By identifying disparities in access, achievement, or support, a needs assessment helps ensure all students have the opportunities to succeed, regardless of their background. It holds the school accountable for continuous improvement, ensuring that any strategic plans are grounded in real needs. Including input from stakeholders like parents and community members creates buy-in and collaboration, which can improve the overall effectiveness of the school's programs.

In essence, conducting a needs assessment ensures that schools are responsive to the specific needs of their students and staff, fostering a culture of continuous improvement and student success.

Shared Leadership Model

Implementing a shared leadership model, where responsibilities and decision-making are distributed among team members, empowers individuals and fosters a sense of ownership. This approach enhances the team's capacity and promotes collaborative decision-making.

"A distributed perspective on leadership acknowledges the work of all individuals who contribute to leadership practice, whether or not they are formally designated or defined as leaders" (Spillane, 2006, p. 15). In Minne-apolis Public Schools, distributed leadership within the curriculum review teams allowed members to take ownership of specific tasks, leading to more efficient and effective decision-making.

Regular Assessments

Regular assessments of the curriculum review team's performance ensure accountability and promote ongoing improvement. These evaluations can include self-assessment, peer feedback, and supervisor evaluations.

"Continuous evaluation ensures accountability and promotes ongoing improvement" (Marzano et al., 2005, p. 64). For instance, in New York City Public Schools, regular assessments helped identify areas for improvement in the review process, leading to better alignment between the selected curriculum and district goals.

Sustaining Team Development

A commitment to continuous improvement and professional growth is essential for high performance. Teams should stay updated with the latest research, trends, and best practices in education, ensuring that their curriculum review process remains current and effective.

"A commitment to continuous learning is essential for sustaining high performance" (Fullan, 2011). In Austin Independent School District, continuous improvement was a key focus, with team members regularly attending conferences and workshops on curriculum innovation.

Conclusion

Building and sustaining effective curriculum review teams ensures high-quality, relevant, and equitable education for all students.

Districts can create curriculum review teams that drive meaningful and lasting change by fostering collaboration, embracing diverse perspectives, and establishing transparent processes. Through professional development, shared leadership, and continuous evaluation, these teams can remain dynamic and practical, ensuring that the curriculum evolves to meet the needs of an ever-changing student population.

Questions for Reflection

To deepen your understanding of how to build and sustain effective curriculum review teams, consider the following questions:

1. How can districts ensure that their curriculum review teams are diverse and representative of the communities they serve?
2. What strategies can be used to foster collaboration and open communication within curriculum review teams?
3. How can professional development support curriculum review teams in evaluating instructional materials for rigor and cultural responsiveness?
4. Why is it essential to implement a shared leadership model within curriculum review teams, and how can this model be effectively structured?
5. What are some practical ways to evaluate the performance of curriculum review teams and ensure continuous improvement?

Bibliography

Fullan, M. (2011). *The moral imperative realized.* Corwin Press.

Marzano, R. J., Waters, T., & McNulty, B. A. (2005). *School leadership that works: From research to results.* ASCD.

Spillane, J. P. (2006). *Distributed leadership.* Jossey-Bass.

CHAPTER SIX

Building Strong Instructional Leaders

In the dynamic and ever-evolving landscape of education, strong leadership teams are essential for driving sustained improvement and fostering a culture of collaboration, innovation, and continuous learning. Effective instructional leadership teams are critical in guiding schools and districts through change, supporting teachers, and ensuring students receive a high-quality education. This chapter explores the principles and practices for building strong leadership teams, emphasizing the importance of collaboration, distributed leadership, and fostering an environment that empowers leaders to drive meaningful change.

Driving School Improvement

Effective leadership is a crucial driver of school improvement. Research shows that "effective leadership is second only to classroom instruction among all school-related factors that contribute to what students learn at school" (Leithwood et al., 2004, p. 5). Strong leadership teams set the tone for school culture, influence instructional practices, and drive efforts toward continuous improvement. By strategically guiding a school or district's vision, goals, and initiatives, leadership teams ensure that improvements are sustained and aligned with student success.

For example, in Long Beach Unified School District, leadership teams played a central role in developing a comprehensive school improvement plan that focused on raising literacy rates across the district. Through collaborative efforts, the leadership team aligned instructional goals with targeted professional development for teachers, resulting in measurable improvements in student achievement.

Fostering a Collaborative Culture

Leadership teams that foster a collaborative culture create environments where teachers, staff, and administrators work together to solve problems, share best practices, and innovate. Collaboration is essential for implementing new strategies and ensuring that initiatives are introduced and effectively integrated into school practice.

"Collaboration among educators is essential for building professional communities that enhance teaching and learning" (DuFour & Fullan, 2013, p. 4). By prioritizing collaboration, leadership teams create a foundation for shared learning, mutual support, and collective problem-solving, which are vital for fostering innovation and sustained progress.

Recruiting and Selecting Leaders

Districts should prioritize diversity in skills, expertise, and experience to build a strong leadership team. A team with varied backgrounds ensures a broad perspective on issues, enhances problem-solving capabilities, and drives innovation.

"Diversity in leadership teams promotes innovation and better decision-making" (Page, 2007). For instance, in the Toronto District School Board, a diverse leadership team brought together instructional leaders, equity specialists, and community liaisons, allowing the district to address a broad range of educational challenges with innovative and equitable solutions.

Commitment to Vision

It is essential to select leaders who are deeply committed to the district's vision and goals. This alignment ensures that all team members are united in purpose and dedicated to advancing the district's mission. Leaders who are committed to the vision help to maintain focus and inspire others to work toward shared objectives.

Leadership Training

Comprehensive leadership training is crucial for developing the skills necessary for effective instructional leadership, such as strategic planning, data analysis, and instructional leadership. Ongoing professional development ensures that leaders can make informed decisions and effectively lead their schools. Often, leaders come from varying instructional backgrounds, and after selecting a new curriculum, the leader is often not part of implementation professional development. This results in placing the majority of outcomes on the teacher, thus creating a fractured responsibility.

"Professional development for school leaders is crucial for building capacity and sustaining improvement" (Darling-Hammond et al., 2010, p. 17). In Washington, D.C. Public Schools, the district implemented a leadership development program focused on instructional leadership and data-driven decision-making which helped school leaders improve teaching quality and student outcomes.

Ongoing Support

Beyond initial training, ongoing support through coaching and mentoring is essential for leadership development. Experienced leaders can guide emerging leaders, fostering their growth and helping them navigate the complexities of school leadership. For example, in the Dallas Independent School District, new principals are paired with veteran leaders for mentorship, providing them with valuable insights and support during their first years in leadership.

Fostering Collaboration

Developing a shared vision and common goals is essential for uniting leadership teams and ensuring all members work toward the same objectives. This alignment provides clarity and direction, empowering the team to collaborate effectively and focus on achieving shared outcomes.

"Few, if any, forces in human affairs are as powerful as shared vision" (Senge, 2006, p. 192). In the case of Montgomery County

Public Schools, the leadership team collaboratively developed a vision for equity in education, aligning their efforts to close achievement gaps and ensure that all students had access to high-quality instruction.

Open Communication

Promoting open and transparent communication within the leadership team fosters trust and collaboration. Regular meetings, collaborative planning sessions, and informal check-ins help maintain strong lines of communication and allow for sharing ideas, challenges, and solutions.

"Open communication is the foundation of effective collaboration" (Garmston & Wellman, 2016, p. 112). For example, leadership teams in Miami-Dade County Public Schools meet regularly to discuss progress on school improvement initiatives, fostering a culture of openness and shared accountability.

Cross-Functional Teams

Forming cross-functional teams with members from different departments and roles leverages diverse perspectives and expertise to address complex challenges. These teams encourage innovation and ensure that leadership decisions consider the varied needs of students, teachers, and the broader community.

Implementing a shared leadership model, where responsibilities and decision-making are distributed among team members, fosters a sense of ownership and accountability at all levels of leadership. This model capitalizes on individual leaders' strengths while enhancing the organization's overall capacity.

"Distributed leadership capitalizes on the strengths of all team members and enhances organizational capacity" (Spillane, 2006, p. 15). For instance, in the Houston Independent School District, the distributed leadership model allowed leadership teams to work collaboratively across schools, sharing strategies for improving student performance and addressing equity issues.

Empowerment Through Autonomy

Providing leadership teams autonomy in decision-making allows them to take ownership of their responsibilities, fostering a culture of innovation and responsiveness. Leaders who feel trusted and empowered are likelier to experiment with new approaches and take calculated risks to improve outcomes. With a robust monitoring system in place, leaders understand the goals and objectives within the context of their schools.

Risk-Taking Culture

Creating a culture that encourages risk-taking and experimentation is essential for fostering innovation within leadership teams. Leaders should feel supported in trying new approaches, learning from failures, and continuously refining their practices.

"Innovation thrives in environments where risk-taking is encouraged and failures are seen as learning opportunities" (Robinson, 2015, p. 118). For example, in the San Diego Unified School District, leadership teams were encouraged to pilot innovative instructional strategies, which led to the successful implementation of new technology-driven learning initiatives.

Resource Allocation

Leadership teams must have access to the resources needed to implement new ideas and initiatives. This includes financial resources, time, and professional development opportunities, critical for empowering leaders to bring their ideas to life.

Regular Assessments

Regular performance evaluations of leadership teams are essential for assessing their effectiveness and ensuring continuous improvement. These evaluations should include self-assessments, peer evaluations, and supervisor feedback, offering a comprehensive view of leadership performance.

"Continuous evaluation of leadership practices is essential for improvement and accountability" (Marzano et al., 2005). In Fairfax County Public Schools, leadership teams undergo regular performance evaluations to align with district goals and progress toward improvement initiatives.

Goal Alignment

Evaluations must be aligned with the district's goals and vision, reinforcing the importance of working towards shared objectives. Leadership effectiveness should be measured based on how thriving teams contribute to achieving the district's mission.

Sustaining Leadership Development

Promoting a culture of continuous learning and professional growth is essential for sustaining leadership effectiveness over time. Leaders should be encouraged to stay updated with the latest research, trends, and best practices in education.

"Lifelong learning is a hallmark of effective leadership" (Fullan, 2011, p. 63). In the Los Angeles Unified School District, leadership teams are regularly provided with opportunities for professional development, including workshops on the latest educational research and leadership practices.

Succession Planning

Succession planning is critical for ensuring continuity of leadership and maintaining progress within the district. By identifying and preparing future leaders, districts can maintain stability and ensure smooth leadership transitions do not disrupt progress.

Conclusion

Building strong instructional leadership teams is essential for fostering collaboration and empowering leaders to drive change effectively within a school district. By recruiting diverse and committed leaders, providing robust professional development, fostering a collaborative culture, distributing leadership responsibilities, and encouraging innovation, districts can create dynamic leadership teams that are well-equipped to navigate the complexities of educational improvement. Continuous evaluation and development ensure that these teams remain effective and adaptive, ultimately enhancing student outcomes and achieving long-term success.

Questions for Reflection

To deepen your understanding of how to build and sustain strong instructional leadership teams, consider the following questions:

1. How can districts recruit and select leaders with diverse skill sets and expertise to form well-rounded leadership teams?
2. What strategies can be used to foster collaboration and open communication within leadership teams?
3. How does providing professional development and ongoing support help leadership teams effectively drive school improvement?
4. Why is distributed leadership important in fostering ownership and accountability within leadership teams?
5. What role does risk-taking play in encouraging innovation within leadership teams, and how can districts support a culture of experimentation?

Bibliography

Darling-Hammond, L., LaPointe, M., Meyerson, D., Orr, M. T., & Cohen, C. (2010). *Preparing principals for a changing world: Lessons from effective school leadership programs.* Jossey-Bass.

DuFour, R., & Fullan, M. (2013). *Cultures built to last: Systemic PLCs at work.* Solution Tree Press.

Fullan, M. (2011). *The moral imperative realized.* Corwin Press.

Garmston, R. J., & Wellman, B. M. (2016). *The adaptive school: A sourcebook for developing collaborative groups.* Rowman & Littlefield.

Leithwood, K., Seashore Louis, K., Anderson, S., & Wahlstrom, K. (2004). *How leadership influences student learning.* Wallace Foundation.

Marzano, R. J., Waters, T., & McNulty, B. A. (2005). *School leadership that works: From research to results*. ASCD.

Page, S. E. (2007). *The difference: How the power of diversity creates better groups, firms, schools, and societies*. Princeton University Press.

Robinson, K. (2015). *Creative schools: The grassroots revolution that's transforming education*. Viking.

Senge, P. M. (2006). *The fifth discipline: The art and practice of the learning organization*. Doubleday.

Spillane, J. P. (2006). *Distributed leadership*. Jossey-Bass.

CHAPTER SEVEN

Developing a Clear Vision and Goals

A clear and compelling vision, supported by well-defined, measurable goals, is essential for driving meaningful and sustainable change within a school district. A vision provides direction, while goals translate that vision into actionable steps, creating a road map for success. By developing a vision that aligns with student needs and stakeholder expectations, districts can guide decision-making, inspire commitment, and ensure that all efforts contribute toward long-term objectives. This chapter explores the process of crafting a vision that inspires and setting goals that are specific, achievable, and aligned with the overarching vision.

Articulate a Vision

For every successful implementation, a clear vision must be articulated across all facets of school systems, from district offices and school sites to classrooms and family and community support structures. Vision statements can be considered your "north star" (Gurley et al., 2015, pp. 217–242). They intend to be the school district's consistent and ongoing directional path. They need to be concise yet all encompassing. They need to reflect the uniqueness of the community and be realistic yet aspirational. They outline the districts' values and objectives. They provide district leaders, school administrators, classroom educators, students, families, and the community a brief but clear overview of the ethos of the entire school system.

In many districts and school systems, vision statements are in place. However, the team's work is to examine existing vision statements, socialize those statements within districts and school systems, and ensure that the vision resonates.

ASK:

- Is our current vision statement alive in all the work that we do at the district, school site, and classroom levels?
- Do our school families, school board, and broader community know and can articulate our vision?
- Have we revisited our vision statement at any point in recent years?
- Does our vision statement reflect the aspirations held for the whole school community? Or does it feel outdated? Generic? Flat? False?

If you've discovered that a re-write of your vision statement is needed, or if your district has yet to clearly articulate a vision that resonates, it's critical to creating the context for successful curriculum implementation that you begin here.

The following guidance offers a process for crafting a vision statement for school districts. Remember that these statements serve as a beacon that guides the whole school community in all that it does, shaping the future for students, staff, and the community. The goal is to create a vision that reflects the districts' shared values and aspirations.

Creating a Vision Statement

1. Start with the Big Picture

Think about what your district wants to achieve for students, educators, and the whole school community. What is it that is envisioned for the district 5, 10, or 20 years from now?

Ask:

- What do we want our students to experience and achieve?
- What kind of environment do we want to create in our schools?
- How will our district contribute to the broader community?

A vision statement is aspirational, so feel free to dream big!

2. Reflect on Core Values

A strong vision is grounded in the district's core values and beliefs. These values provide the foundation for the district's work and guide its long-term objectives. Identify and articulate the core values underpinning the district's efforts, such as equity, excellence, and inclusivity. According to Senge (2006, p. 192), "A shared vision is not an idea . . . it is, rather, a force in people's hearts." These values should resonate with the entire community and drive the district's commitment to student success. Ensure that the vision reflects the cultural diversity of the district's student population and the broader community. A culturally relevant vision acknowledges and embraces diversity, fostering a sense of belonging and inclusion for all stakeholders.

Ask:

- Inclusivity and equity for all students?
- A commitment to excellence and innovation?
- Building strong relationships with families and the community?

When writing the vision, it's important to reflect those values. Let them shine through!

3. Think About Students' Futures

Ultimately, your vision should serve students. Think about the kind of future you want to prepare them for.

Ask:

- What skills and qualities will help students thrive in a rapidly changing world?
- How can we empower students to be compassionate, engaged, and responsible citizens?
- How can we nurture not only academic success but also personal growth and well-being?

Your district's vision should focus on preparing students for success, both in school and beyond.

4. Keep It Clear and Inspiring

A great vision statement is both clear and inspiring. It should be easy to understand while capturing the hopes and dreams that you have for your district. Here are a few tips to keep in mind:

- Use simple, positive language that everyone—students, parents, teachers—can connect with.
- Focus on the future by highlighting what you aim to achieve together.
- Make it meaningful by using words that resonate with your community and reflect your shared aspirations.

A well-written vision statement should leave everyone feeling inspired and excited about the future.

> *"Students are curious, engaged learners who gain the tools and knowledge to become positive contributing members of local and global communities. Our universally designed, personalized, flexible, inclusive, tiered instructional model includes a rich, rigorous, comprehensive, and aligned curriculum measured by authentic assessments. We employ strong professionals who are enabled by continuous training and support to make decisions based on expertise, data, and research. The schools are physically and emotionally safe spaces."*

Figure 7.1. Sample Vision

Engaging Stakeholders

A vision is most effective when it reflects the aspirations and values of the entire school community. Engaging stakeholders in the visioning process ensures that the vision is inclusive and widely supported.

Involve a diverse group of stakeholders, including students, parents, teachers, administrators, and community members. This ensures that the vision reflects a broad range of perspectives and needs. "Stakeholder engagement is crucial for developing a vision that is inclusive and widely supported" (Fullan, 2007). For example, a district might conduct listening sessions and workshops to gather input from various groups on their hopes and priorities for the future.

Facilitate workshops and focus groups to build consensus around the vision. These discussions allow stakeholders to explore their aspirations for the district's future. This collaborative approach can help identify common themes and establish a shared direction.

Refining and Communicating the Vision

Once a draft vision statement has been developed, it is important to refine it based on feedback and communicate it clearly to all stakeholders. Share the draft vision statement with stakeholders and solicit feedback. This iterative process helps ensure the vision resonates with the broader community and accurately reflects their aspirations. Develop a communication plan to disseminate the vision throughout the district. Use channels—staff meetings, newsletters, social media, and the district's website—to reach all stakeholders. Consistent messaging ensures that everyone is aligned with the vision.

Aligning Goals With the Vision

A district's goals must directly support the achievement of the vision. Each goal represents a concrete step toward realizing the broader aspirations outlined in the vision statement.

All goals should align with the district's vision, ensuring that every initiative and action contributes to the overall objectives. For example, if the vision focuses on equity, goals might include reducing achievement gaps or increasing access to advanced coursework for underrepresented students.

Identify the strategic priorities that will guide goal setting. These priorities should reflect the most critical areas for improvement and growth, ensuring that resources and efforts are directed where needed.

Goal-Setting Process

The process of setting goals should be data driven and collaborative. Use data to inform goal setting. Analyzing academic performance, behavioral trends, and stakeholder feedback helps identify the areas that require the most attention. For instance, data might suggest focusing on targeted interventions in a district with declining math scores in early grades.

Involve stakeholders in the goal-setting process. Engaging teachers, administrators, parents, and students in discussions around goals promotes ownership and accountability. This collaboration ensures that the goals are realistic, grounded in the district's context, and supported by the community.

Action Plans and Implementation

Once goals are established, districts need to develop action plans that outline the steps required to achieve them. Action plans should clearly outline the steps needed to achieve each goal. This includes specifying timelines, assigning responsibilities, and identifying required resources. "An action plan provides the roadmap for achieving goals and ensures that all efforts are aligned and coordinated" (Kotter, 1996, p. 101). For instance, an action plan to improve literacy rates might include professional development for teachers, implementing new instructional materials, and regular assessments.

Ensure that the necessary financial, human, and material resources are allocated to support achieving goals. This may require reallocating existing resources or seeking additional funding to meet the district's needs.

Monitoring and Evaluation

Ongoing monitoring and evaluation are essential for tracking progress and ensuring continuous improvement. Establish regular check-ins to review progress toward goals. Use these opportunities to assess what is working, identify challenges, and make necessary adjustments to the action plans. To evaluate progress, use a combination of formative and summative assessments. Tracking both short-term milestones and long-term outcomes allows districts to gauge the effectiveness of their strategies and make data-informed decisions.

Foster a culture of continuous improvement by using evaluation data to refine strategies and practices. Constant monitoring and adjustment ensure that goals remain relevant and achievable as circumstances change.

Transparent Communication

Clear and transparent communication throughout the process helps keep stakeholders informed and engaged. Regularly update stakeholders on progress, challenges, and successes. Transparency helps maintain trust and ensures everyone remains aligned with the district's objectives.

Establish mechanisms for stakeholders to provide ongoing feedback. This will allow the district to make adjustments based on input from the community and ensure that the vision and goals continue to resonate with the school community.

Conclusion

Developing a clear vision and setting measurable goals are critical steps in driving meaningful change within a school district. A compelling vision, grounded in shared values and crafted through stakeholder collaboration, provides the foundation for all district initiatives. Setting specific, achievable, and aligned goals ensures the vision is translated into actionable steps guiding the district's work. Engaging stakeholders in visioning and goal setting promotes broad-based support, while continuous monitoring and evaluation foster a culture of improvement. Ultimately, this strategic approach inspires and unites the community in pursuing excellence and equity for all students.

Questions for Reflection

To deepen your understanding of how to develop a clear vision and measurable goals, consider the following questions:

1. How can engaging a diverse group of stakeholders in the visioning process help create a more inclusive and widely supported vision?

2. Why is it important to align goals with the district's vision, and how can districts ensure their goals are both ambitious and achievable?
3. What role do action plans play in achieving district goals, and how can districts ensure they allocate resources effectively?
4. How can regular monitoring and evaluation help districts stay on track and continuously improve their strategies and practices?

Bibliography

Fullan, M. (2007). *The new meaning of educational change*. Teachers College Press.

Gurley, D. K., Peters, G. B., Collins, L., & Fifolt, M. (2015). Mission, vision, values, and goals: An exploration of key organizational statements and daily practice in schools. *Journal of Educational Change, 16*(2), 217–242. https://doi.org/10.1007/s10833-014-9229-x

Kotter, J. P. (1996). *Leading change*. Harvard Business Review Press.

Senge, P. M. (2006). *The fifth discipline: The art and practice of the learning organization*. Doubleday.

CHAPTER EIGHT

Case Studies

Enabling context is a critical component of Implementation Science, as it refers to the conditions and support systems that must be in place to ensure the successful adoption and sustainability of evidence-based practices. This includes creating an environment where resources, leadership, organizational culture, and stakeholder engagement align to support the implementation process. An enabling context ensures that schools and districts are prepared to introduce new programs or curricula, maintain integrity and fidelity, address challenges, and adapt as necessary. Strong leadership, ongoing professional development, clear communication, and a collaborative culture are crucial elements that foster an enabling context. Without these, even the best-designed interventions are likely to falter. Understanding how to cultivate and sustain this context is essential before examining case studies that illustrate successful applications of Implementation Science in real-world educational settings.

Case Studies and Examples

Example 1: Cross-Functional Curriculum Review Team in a Suburban District

In a suburban district in Illinois, a cross-functional curriculum review team was formed to overhaul the district's instructional materials and curricula. The team included teachers from various subject areas, school administrators, and parents, ensuring that multiple perspectives were considered in the decision-making process.

The district created a more cohesive and integrated curriculum across grade levels by bringing together stakeholders from different departments and backgrounds. The collaboration between teachers from other subject areas led to a more interdisciplinary approach to instruction, allowing students to engage with material more interconnectedly.

"The cross-functional team approach allowed us to leverage diverse expertise and create a more comprehensive curriculum" (Choi & Drago-Severson, 2023). This example highlights the importance of cross-functional collaboration in creating curricular cohesion and ensuring that instructional materials meet the needs of all students.

Case Studies and Examples: Collaboration and Leadership

Example 1: District-Wide Professional Learning Communities in a Large Urban District

A large urban school district in New York faced significant disparities in student outcomes across its schools. To address this challenge, the district implemented district-wide Professional Learning Communities (PLCs) that fostered collaboration among school leaders, teachers, and administrators. The PLCs provided a structured environment where educators could share best practices, discuss common challenges, and collaborate on solutions.

As a result, the district saw significant improvements in student outcomes, particularly in math and literacy. The collaboration within the PLCs allowed schools to address gaps in instruction, support struggling students more effectively, and refine teaching practices.

"The success of our PLCs lies in the shared commitment to continuous improvement and the collective responsibility for student success" (Johnson, 2021, p. 52). This case demonstrates how fostering collaboration through PLCs can lead to more effective problem-solving and improvements in student achievement across an entire district.

Example 2: Distributed Leadership in Action in a Suburban District

A suburban school district in Texas adopted a distributed leadership model to empower teachers to take on key roles in decision-making processes. Rather than concentrating leadership in the hands of a few administrators, the district encouraged teachers to assume leadership roles in areas such as curriculum development, professional development, and student support services. This distributed leadership model was aligned with the principles of Implementation Science, as it sought to build leadership capacity across the district and empower those closest to the work of teaching and learning.

The impact of this approach was profound. Teacher leaders played a significant role in introducing innovative solutions to instructional challenges, leading to higher engagement levels among teachers and students. The shared responsibility also fostered a stronger sense of ownership and accountability among staff.

"Empowering teacher leaders has transformed our district's approach to problem-solving and innovation" (Smith, 2021, p. 122). This case illustrates how distributed leadership can enhance the capacity of a district to address complex problems, foster innovation, and engage teachers more deeply in school improvement.

Lessons Learned From Implementation Science Successes

The successes of these districts and schools demonstrate several critical lessons about the practical application of Implementation Science principles in education:

1. **Inclusion and Stakeholder Engagement:** Engaging diverse stakeholders in decision-making processes—whether through inclusive curriculum review or distributed leadership—ensures that diverse perspectives are considered, leading to more relevant and effective outcomes. Involving students, parents, teachers, and community members enriches decision-making and enhances buy-in.
2. **Collaboration and Cross-Functional Teams:** Collaboration across different roles and departments—whether through PLCs or cross-functional teams—promotes knowledge sharing and allows districts to leverage a variety of expertise to solve problems. Structured collaboration through PLCs or cross-functional teams fosters a shared sense of responsibility and helps break down silos within schools and districts.

3. **Leadership Development and Distribution:** Distributed leadership models that empower teachers to take on leadership roles build capacity and foster a culture of innovation. By distributing leadership responsibilities, districts enhance the effectiveness of their initiatives and promote teacher engagement and ownership of school improvement efforts.
4. **Cultural Responsiveness:** Implementing culturally responsive practices, as seen in the inclusive curriculum review example, is essential for addressing students' diverse needs. This requires thoughtful and inclusive planning involving underrepresented voices in decision-making processes.

Conclusion

Implementation Science offers a robust framework for driving meaningful and sustainable change within schools and districts. By applying the principles of stakeholder engagement, collaboration, distributed leadership, and cultural responsiveness principles, educational institutions across the United States have significantly improved student outcomes. The case studies highlighted in this chapter demonstrate the potential of Implementation Science to transform educational practices at the state, district, and school levels, fostering more inclusive, collaborative, and practical approaches to teaching and learning.

By building on these successes, other districts and schools can apply the lessons of Implementation Science to their own contexts, ensuring that educational initiatives are implemented, sustained, and continuously improved over time.

Questions for Reflection

To deepen your understanding of the role of Implementation Science in driving educational success, consider the following questions:

1. How can engaging diverse stakeholders in decision-making contribute to more effective and inclusive educational outcomes?

2. Why are cross-functional teams and PLCs essential for fostering collaboration and improving teaching and learning across a district?
3. How does distributed leadership empower teachers and contribute to school and district improvement efforts?
4. What are the key benefits of implementing culturally responsive practices in curriculum development, and how can districts ensure that their curriculum reflects the diversity of their student population?
5. How can the principles of Implementation Science be applied in your school or district to foster innovation, collaboration, and sustained improvement?

Bibliography

Choi, H., & Drago-Severson, E. (2023). Helping teacher leadership teams: Enhancing teaming by focusing knowledge integration. *European Journal of Educational Management, 6*(2), 69–82.

Johnson, S. (2021). *Local assessments an option if statewide tests aren't viable during pandemic, California official signal.* EdSource. https://edsource.org/2021/california-school-districts-get-ok-to-choose-localassessments-over-statewide-tests-this-spring/652435

Smith, A. (2021). Empowering teacher leaders: A case study in distributed leadership. *Journal of Educational Change, 6*(1), 122–127.

PART IV

Effective Practices

The success of any educational initiative hinges not only on its initial implementation but also on the ability to continuously assess its impact and make necessary adjustments. Without a structured system for monitoring progress, even the most well-intentioned programs may fall short of their intended goals. Effective monitoring systems allow school districts to track key performance indicators, evaluate the efficacy of interventions, and ensure that resources are being allocated efficiently to maximize student outcomes.

Implementation Science provides a structured approach to ensuring that evidence-based educational strategies are successfully adopted, implemented, and sustained in schools and districts. At its core, successful implementation is not simply about choosing the right intervention, it is about creating the conditions, structures, and habits that allow that intervention to take root and thrive. This requires a focus on effective practices, the key actions and systems that ensure schools move from planning to execution and from short-term change to long-term transformation.

Effective practices are a critical component of the Implementation Science formula, ensuring that an initiative is not just introduced but monitored, adapted, institutionalized, and celebrated in ways that drive continuous improvement. Without these practices in place, even the most well-researched and promising educational strategies may struggle to gain traction or fade away due to lack of support, engagement, or alignment with district priorities.

This section explores four foundational aspects of effective practices that are essential for sustaining educational improvement:

1. **Monitoring Progress and Adapting Strategies:** Establishing data-driven systems that track implementation success, identify areas for improvement, and ensure real-time adjustments that enhance outcomes.

2. **Ensuring Usable and Scalable Innovations:** Designing and refining interventions so they are clear, adaptable, and replicable across various educational settings without losing their core impact.
3. **Engaging Stakeholders for Lasting Impact:** Building strong partnerships with educators, parents, students, and community members to secure buy-in, leverage resources, and ensure long-term sustainability.
4. **Celebrating Success and Sustaining Momentum:** Recognizing achievements, embedding successful practices into district culture, and maintaining enthusiasm for ongoing improvement.

Each of these areas will be explored in depth in the following chapters, providing a roadmap for instructional leaders to ensure that the work they do results in meaningful, enduring change.

Monitoring Progress and Adapting Strategies

One of the biggest challenges in educational reform is ensuring that initiatives do not just get launched but also stay on track and continuously improve. Too often, schools implement new programs without robust mechanisms to evaluate progress or adjust course when needed. Monitoring progress and adapting strategies are essential to bridge the gap between implementation and impact.

A strong monitoring system allows educators to:

- Assess the effectiveness of new interventions using real-time data.
- Identify challenges early and address them before they derail progress.
- Ensure accountability by aligning implementation with clearly defined goals.
- Make informed decisions that are rooted in evidence rather than assumptions.

One of the most effective frameworks for continuous monitoring is the Plan-Do-Study-Act (PDSA) cycle, which supports iterative learning and adjustment. This model ensures that implementation is not static but responsive, allowing districts to refine strategies based on student outcomes, teacher feedback, and contextual needs.

Additionally, data-driven decision-making must go beyond test scores. Districts should integrate multiple forms of data, including classroom observations, student engagement metrics, and qualitative feedback from educators and families. By making data accessible, actionable, and transparent, school leaders can foster a culture of continuous improvement where adaptation is seen as a strength rather than a sign of failure.

Ensuring Usable and Scalable Innovations

For an initiative to be effective, it must be usable and scalable across different educational settings. Many programs fail because they are too complex, loosely defined, or difficult to replicate in diverse schools and classrooms. Usable innovations must have:

- **A Clear Description:** Clearly defined objectives, principles, and intended outcomes that provide a shared understanding of the intervention.
- **Defined Essential Functions:** Core components that must be present for the intervention to achieve its intended impact.
- **Operational Definitions:** Specific, observable indicators that ensure consistency in implementation across different sites.
- **Practical Performance Assessments:** Systems to measure fidelity and effectiveness in real-world conditions.

For example, a literacy intervention rooted in the Science of Reading should have clear guidelines on phonics instruction, structured lesson delivery, and formative assessments. If these elements are clearly outlined and embedded into professional development and instructional coaching, schools are far more likely to see consistent, positive results.

Additionally, usability does not mean rigidity. While fidelity to core components is crucial, districts must also build in flexibility to accommodate different student populations, school cultures, and resource constraints. The most successful educational interventions are those that strike a balance between consistency and adaptability.

Engaging Stakeholders for Lasting Impact

Educational change does not happen in isolation. Without the support and engagement of key stakeholders, even the most promising initiatives can stall or face resistance. Engaging stakeholders is about building a coalition of support that includes teachers, administrators, students, parents, and community partners.

Key strategies for effective stakeholder engagement include:

- **Building Buy-In Early:** Involving teachers and administrators in the selection and design of new initiatives to ensure alignment with instructional priorities and classroom realities.
- **Creating Teacher Leadership Roles:** Empowering educators to lead implementation efforts fosters peer collaboration and increases the likelihood of success.
- **Establishing Parent and Community Partnerships:** Parents and community organizations can provide additional resources, advocacy, and support to sustain initiatives beyond the school walls.
- **Transparent Communication:** Keeping stakeholders informed through regular updates, data-sharing, and open forums for feedback ensures that everyone feels invested in the process.

When stakeholders are actively engaged rather than passively informed, initiatives are more likely to succeed because they reflect the voices, needs, and expertise of the communities they serve.

Celebrating Success and Sustaining Momentum

Sustaining change requires more than just good planning. Schools and districts must actively recognize progress, reinforce effective practices, and create structures that ensure long-term sustainability. Without reinforcement, initiatives can lose momentum and educators may revert to old habits.

Celebrating success plays a crucial role in maintaining enthusiasm and commitment. Effective strategies include:

- **Formal Recognition Programs:** Establishing awards for educators, administrators, and students who exemplify the goals of the initiative.
- **Public Showcasing of Achievements:** Sharing success stories through newsletters, social media, and community events.
- **Institutionalizing Effective Practices:** Embedding successful interventions into district policies, professional development programs, and instructional frameworks to ensure they are not dependent on individual leaders or short-term funding.

By acknowledging the work and dedication of educators and students, districts can create a culture where improvement is not just mandated but celebrated. This fosters pride, motivation, and a shared sense of purpose that sustains momentum over time.

This chapter explores the essential components of a robust monitoring system, the strategies for leveraging data to drive meaningful change, and how districts can implement sustainable processes that ensure long-term educational success. Through proactive assessment and adaptive leadership, schools can create dynamic learning environments where every student has the opportunity to thrive.

CHAPTER NINE

Monitoring and Adapting Strategies

School districts must establish robust systems to monitor progress and adapt strategies based on data-driven insights for educational initiatives to succeed. Monitoring systems are critical in helping districts assess their program's effectiveness, identify improvement areas, and ensure that resources are used efficiently to maximize student outcomes. This chapter explores the importance of continuous monitoring, the components of an effective monitoring system, strategies for data-informed adaptation, and how districts can create systems that drive meaningful, sustainable improvement.

Continuous Improvement

Continuous improvement is the backbone of any successful educational initiative. Regular monitoring allows districts to gather essential feedback to make informed decisions about program adjustments, instructional strategies, and resource allocations.

"Continuous monitoring provides the feedback necessary for educational leaders to make data-driven decisions that enhance student learning and system efficiency" (Mandinach & Gummer, 2016). This process involves tracking progress, analyzing data, and making iterative changes that foster an environment of constant learning and development. For instance, schools implementing a new reading curriculum can use frequent assessments to determine how well students are progressing and adjust instruction as needed to better support those struggling.

Accountability

Monitoring systems also play a crucial role in fostering accountability within education. They ensure that educators and administrators are held accountable for student outcomes and that districts remain responsive to their students' needs.

"Accountability in education helps ensure that all students receive a quality education and that educators and administrators are responsive to student needs" (Darling-Hammond, 2010, p. 30). By measuring performance against clearly defined goals and standards, districts can demonstrate their commitment to continuous improvement and equity in education.

Building Effective Monitoring Systems

Establishing Clear Metrics and Goals

The foundation of any effective monitoring system is the establishment of clear, measurable goals that align with the district's broader objectives.

- **Goal Alignment:** Goals should be aligned with district objectives and serve as benchmarks for monitoring progress. SMART goals—Specific, Measurable, Achievable, Relevant, and Time-bound—are particularly effective for guiding monitoring efforts. "Goals should be SMART to effectively guide monitoring efforts" (Doran, 1981, pp. 35–36). For example, a district aiming to improve student attendance might set a SMART goal to increase overall attendance rates by 5% within the next academic year.
- **Selection of Metrics:** Choosing the right metrics is essential to accurately reflect the critical aspects of programs and strategies being implemented. These metrics might include student achievement data, graduation rates, attendance records, and other indicators of educational quality. Effective metrics provide a comprehensive picture of progress and help pinpoint areas in need of improvement.

Data Collection and Management

Efficient data collection and management are vital components of a monitoring system. Districts must establish processes for collecting both quantitative and qualitative data from various sources.

- **Comprehensive Data Collection:** A robust monitoring system captures a wide range of indicators, including academic performance, behavioral data, and feedback from students, parents, and educators. "Effective data collection is comprehensive, capturing a range of indicators from academic performance to student and community feedback" (Bernhardt, 2013, p. 9). For instance, a district implementing a new math intervention could collect data on student test scores, teacher feedback on curriculum effectiveness, and parent input on student engagement.
- **Data Management Systems:** Once data are collected, they need to be organized, stored, and analyzed efficiently. Data management systems that enable timely access to insights are essential for driving informed decision-making. "Advanced data systems enable more sophisticated analysis and more responsive educational practices" (Wayman, 2005, p. 295). These systems should allow for easy data entry, retrieval, and analysis, helping educators make sense of the data and use it to guide their practice.

Strategies for Data-Informed Adaptation

Data Analysis and Reporting

Once data have been collected and managed, regular analysis is necessary to assess progress against goals and inform strategic adjustments.

- **Regular Data Analysis:** Districts should conduct regular analyses to identify trends, assess the effectiveness of interventions, and make informed decisions about where to allocate resources. This process involves comparing current data with historical benchmarks and identifying areas that require further attention. "Ongoing analysis helps identify trends that inform strategic adjustments and resource allocation" (Ikemoto & Marsh, 2007).

- **Accessible Reporting:** Reporting data in a clear, accessible manner is essential for engaging stakeholders and fostering transparency. Reports should be designed to communicate key findings to a wide audience, including school boards, teachers, parents, and students. "Transparency in data reporting fosters trust and engagement from the community and enhances the accountability of educational systems" (Kowalski et al., 2008, p. 47). For example, creating user-friendly dashboards that summarize key performance metrics allows stakeholders to easily understand progress and take action where needed.

Engaging Stakeholders in the Review Process

Engaging a diverse range of stakeholders in the monitoring and review process is critical for ensuring that strategies remain relevant and responsive to student needs.

- **Stakeholder Engagement:** Involving teachers, students, parents, and community members in reviewing progress ensures that monitoring efforts are well-rounded and contextually informed. "Engagement with a broad range of stakeholders enriches the review process and supports more effective adaptations" (Bryk et al., 2010). For instance, holding regular review meetings with parents and community leaders allows for the incorporation of diverse perspectives and experiences, which can enhance the effectiveness of interventions.
- **Feedback Mechanisms:** Implementing formal feedback mechanisms helps districts collect ongoing input from stakeholders and refine strategies as needed. Surveys, focus groups, and direct communication channels provide avenues for stakeholders to share their experiences and offer suggestions for improvement. "Feedback is a powerful tool for improvement, providing a direct line to stakeholder experiences and perceptions" (Hattie, 2009). This feedback loop is essential for continuously adapting and refining educational strategies.

Adapting Strategies Based on Monitoring

Iterative Process

Effective adaptation requires an iterative process where districts continuously refine their strategies based on data insights.

- **Responsive Adjustments:** Adaptation requires districts to be flexible and responsive to the data they collect. Timely adjustments to strategies help districts address emerging challenges and capitalize on opportunities to enhance student outcomes. "Adaptation is key to ensuring that educational strategies remain effective and responsive to student needs" (Fullan, 2007, p. 54). For instance, if data reveal that a reading intervention is not working as intended for a subset of students, educators might modify the approach or provide additional supports to meet those students' needs better.

Conclusion

Monitoring progress and adapting strategies based on data-driven insights are critical to effective educational management. Robust monitoring systems allow districts to assess the effectiveness of their programs, ensure accountability, and make informed decisions that drive continuous improvement. By establishing clear metrics, collecting comprehensive data, engaging stakeholders, and utilizing adaptive strategies, districts can ensure that their educational initiatives are effective and responsive to the evolving needs of their students. Continuous monitoring and adaptation foster a culture of excellence and accountability, leading to better student outcomes.

Questions for Reflection

To deepen your understanding of monitoring systems and data-informed adaptation in education, consider the following questions:

1. How can districts ensure that their goals and metrics are aligned with broader district objectives and effectively guide monitoring efforts?

2. What are the benefits of using both quantitative and qualitative data to monitor the effectiveness of educational programs?
3. How can districts effectively engage a diverse range of stakeholders in the monitoring and review process, and why is this important?
4. What challenges might districts face in adapting strategies based on monitoring data, and how can they address these challenges to ensure that their interventions remain effective?

Bibliography

Bernhardt, V. L. (2013). *Data analysis for continuous school improvement*. Routledge.

Bryk, A. S., Sebring, P. B., Allensworth, E., Luppescu, S., & Easton, J. Q. (2010). *Organizing schools for improvement: Lessons from Chicago*. University of Chicago Press.

Darling-Hammond, L. (2010). *The flat world and education: How America's commitment to equity will determine our future*. Teachers College Press.

Doran, G. T. (1981). There's a S.M.A.R.T. way to write management's goals and objectives. *Management Review, 70*(11), 35–36.

Fullan, M. (2007). *The new meaning of educational change*. Teachers College Press.

Hattie, J. (2009). *Visible learning: A synthesis of over 800 meta-analyses relating to achievement*. Routledge.

Ikemoto, G. S., & Marsh, J. A. (2007). Cutting through the "data-driven" mantra: Different conceptions of data-driven decision making. *Yearbook of the National Society for the Study of Education, 106*(1), 105–131.

Kowalski, T. J., Lasley, T. J., & Mahoney, J. W. (2008). *Data-driven decision making in the classroom: Pedagogical and instructional considerations*. Allyn & Bacon.

Mandinach, E. B., & Gummer, E. S. (2016). *Data literacy for educators: Making it count in teacher preparation and practice*. Teachers College Press.

Wayman, J. C. (2005). Involving teachers in data-driven decision making: Using computer data systems to support teacher inquiry and reflection. *Journal of Education for Students Placed at Risk, 10*(3), 295–308.

CHAPTER TEN

Usable Innovations

Implementing any educational program or intervention requires careful planning, clear goals, and an in-depth understanding of the essential elements that make the innovation effective. Usable innovations can be consistently applied across settings, yielding reliable results aligned with the program's intended outcomes. Specific criteria must be in place to ensure that an educational program or practice is usable, including a clear program description, well-defined essential functions, operational definitions, and practical performance assessments. By adhering to these criteria, educators and leaders can effectively replicate and scale innovations across schools and districts, fostering greater consistency, accountability, and long-term success.

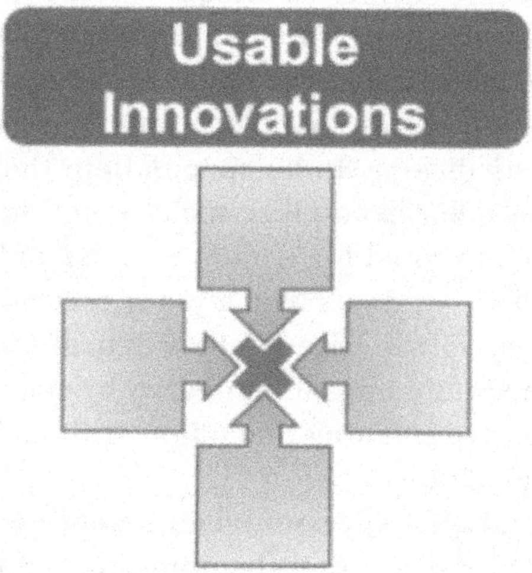

Figure 10.1. Usable Innovation

Fixsen, D. L., & Blase, K. A. (2020). Active implementation frameworks. In P. Nilsen & S. A. Birken (Eds.), *Handbook on implementation science* (pp. 62–68). Edward Elgar Publishing.

A clear description is foundational to any usable innovation, as it outlines the philosophy, values, principles, and target population for whom the program is designed. The program description not only serves as a blueprint but also establishes a shared understanding among all stakeholders, guiding implementation and helping align the program with the district's broader goals.

An educational program's underlying philosophy, values, and principles are essential because they communicate the purpose and vision of the innovation. These elements provide a "north star" for all implementation efforts, ensuring that the program's core mission remains clear even as it is adapted to fit various contexts. For example, a literacy intervention grounded in the Science of Reading should reflect values like evidence-based instruction, inclusivity, and a commitment to closing achievement gaps in literacy. According to Fixsen et al. (2005), grounding innovations in a core set of values and principles facilitates the creation of a consistent program that resonates across different classrooms and communities, as it reinforces shared goals and expectations.

Clearly defining the population for which the program is intended is critical to ensuring its effectiveness. Inclusion and exclusion criteria help educators determine who will benefit most from the program and avoid implementing it in settings or with students for whom it may not be suitable. This clarity is especially important when working with diverse student populations that may have different learning needs. For example, a social-emotional learning (SEL) program may be designed for students at risk of behavioral issues but not intended for students who already receive intensive behavioral interventions. Clear criteria allow educators to use resources effectively and maintain program integrity by ensuring that the program is implemented in a way that aligns with its intended purpose (Greenhalgh et al., 2004).

Identifying and defining essential functions—often referred to as core components—ensures that the innovation remains intact, even when it is adapted to suit specific contexts. Core components are the nonnegotiable aspects of a program that drive its success, and they play a critical role in improving implementation efficiency, supporting evaluations, and facilitating consistent outcomes.

Core components should reflect the fundamental aspects of the program that are directly linked to its intended outcomes. For example, in a literacy intervention, core components might include explicit phonics instruction, regular formative assessments, and differentiated support for struggling readers. Establishing these components ensures that, regardless of the setting, the essential aspects of the program are consistently applied, improving both efficiency and effectiveness of implementation (Odom et al., 2010). Core components also support evaluation by providing specific elements to measure, allowing leaders to determine whether the program is being implemented as intended.

Clearly defined core components help streamline the implementation process by reducing ambiguity and minimizing the need for constant decision-making on what should or should not be included in the program. When essential functions are well-articulated, they serve as a guide for educators, enhancing the likelihood that the program will be implemented effectively and efficiently. As a result, teachers can spend less time navigating ambiguous expectations and more time focusing on high-impact instructional practices (Fixsen et al., 2013).

Core components are also essential for evaluating program implementation. By defining what constitutes "full" or "high-fidelity" implementation, districts can assess how well the program is being carried out in various settings. For instance, the National Implementation Research Network (NIRN) emphasizes that well-defined core components enable consistent monitoring and provide a baseline for measuring program fidelity, which is necessary for assessing program effectiveness (NIRN, 2020b).

Operational Definitions of Essential Functions

For a program to be usable and scalable, its essential functions must have clear, operational definitions. Operational definitions describe how each core component is manifested in practice, offering concrete indicators that can be observed, measured, and replicated across multiple settings. These definitions foster consistency and allow for scalability.

Operational definitions provide specific criteria or indicators for each core component, making it easier to assess whether these components are being implemented as intended. This approach is supported by Joyce and Showers (2002), who emphasized the importance of clearly defined practices for ensuring consistent implementation and promoting educator accountability. These clear indicators help ensure that educators understand what is expected, creating a foundation for consistent and high-fidelity implementation. For instance, if a core component is "regular formative assessment," the operational definition might specify that teachers conduct assessments biweekly, record results in a standardized format, and use the data to adjust instructional strategies.

Operational definitions are essential for promoting consistency across classrooms, schools, and districts. When core components are uniformly defined and operationalized, educators across different settings can adhere to a common standard, leading to more reliable results. Research suggests that consistency is crucial for achieving equitable outcomes in education, as it reduces variability in how students experience the program (Durlak & DuPre, 2008). Operational definitions also ensure that the program's impact is not diluted as it is implemented at scale, preserving its effectiveness across diverse contexts.

Operational definitions support scalability by making it easier for districts to replicate the program across multiple sites. By clearly defining the "how" of implementation, districts can train educators effectively, monitor fidelity, and identify any deviations from the intended model. This structured approach not only enables replication but also facilitates the identification and resolution of challenges that may arise during scale-up efforts, helping to maintain the program's integrity as it expands (Fixsen et al., 2013).

Practical Performance Assessment

Finally, practical performance assessments grounded in the core components of the program are necessary to determine whether the innovation is effective when used as intended. Performance assessments provide evidence of the program's success and help identify areas for improvement.

Performance assessments should be directly linked to the core components of the program to ensure that they accurately measure implementation fidelity and program impact. For example, if a core component of a math intervention is the use of manipulatives to teach number sense, the performance assessment should include metrics on how frequently and effectively these tools are used in the classroom. By aligning assessment tools with the program's essential functions, districts can gather meaningful data that reflect the program's implementation and outcomes (Dane & Schneider, 1998).

To support long-term sustainability, performance assessments should be practical, manageable, and able to be conducted at multiple levels of the educational system. Regular, repeatable assessments allow educators and administrators to monitor implementation progress, identify trends, and make necessary adjustments. For instance, quick surveys, classroom observations, and review of student work samples can be integrated into routine practices, providing ongoing feedback without creating excessive burdens for staff (Scheirer & Dearing, 2011).

Performance assessments offer valuable evidence regarding the program's effectiveness. When assessments consistently show positive student outcomes aligned with the program's goals, educators and leaders can be confident in the innovation's value. However, suppose assessments indicate areas where the program is not yielding expected results. In that case, this evidence can prompt adjustments to the implementation or core components, ensuring that the program remains responsive to student needs. Regular assessments thus play a crucial role in maintaining program relevance and effectiveness over time (Proctor et al., 2011).

Conclusion

Creating a usable innovation requires more than just selecting an evidence-based program; it involves a structured approach to ensure that the program can be consistently implemented, scaled, and evaluated across different settings. By focusing on a clear program description, well-defined essential functions, operational definitions, and practical performance assessments, educators can create a robust framework that supports the long-term success and sustainability of the program. These elements of usability not only foster consistency and accountability but also empower educators to implement interventions with confidence and purpose, leading to meaningful and sustainable improvements in student outcomes.

Questions for Reflection

To further your understanding, consider the following questions:

1. How clearly does our program's description communicate its philosophy, values, and intended impact on students and staff?
2. What essential functions and core components of the program are nonnegotiable for achieving our desired outcomes?
3. Are our core components well-defined with operational indicators that can be consistently observed and measured?
4. In what ways can our performance assessments be practical and sustainable, allowing for ongoing evaluation without creating burdens on staff?
5. How might the inclusion and exclusion criteria for this program ensure it serves the intended population effectively?
6. What steps can we take to ensure that our implementation practices allow for scalability and adaptability while maintaining program fidelity?

Bibliography

Dane, A. V., & Schneider, B. H. (1998). Program integrity in primary and early secondary prevention: Are implementation effects out of control? *Clinical Psychology Review, 18*(1), 23–45.

Durlak, J. A., & DuPre, E. P. (2008). Implementation matters: A review of research on the influence of implementation on program outcomes and the factors affecting implementation. *American Journal of Community Psychology, 41*(3–4), 327–350.

Fixsen, D. L., Blase, K. A., Metz, A., & Van Dyke, M. K. (2013). Statewide implementation of evidence-based programs. *Exceptional Children, 79*(2), 213–230.

Fixsen, D. L., Naoom, S. F., Blase, K. A., Friedman, R. M., & Wallace, F. (2005). *Implementation research: A synthesis of the literature.* University of South Florida, Louis de la Parte Florida Mental Health Institute, The National Implementation Research Network.

Greenhalgh, T., Robert, G., Macfarlane, F., Bate, P., & Kyriakidou, O. (2004). Diffusion of innovations in service organizations: Systematic review and recommendations. *The Milbank Quarterly, 82*(4), 581–629.

Joyce, B., & Showers, B. (2002). *Student achievement through staff development.* (3rd ed.). Association for Supervision and Curriculum Development.

National Implementation Research Network (NIRN). (2020a). *Framework for effective implementation.* University of North Carolina at Chapel Hill.

National Implementation Research Network (NIRN). (2020b). *Usable innovations: Handout10.* University of North Carolina at Chapel Hill. https://nirn.fpg.unc.edu/sites/nirn.fpg.unc.edu/files/resources/AIHub-Handout10-UsableInnovations.pdf

Odom, S. L., Cox, A. W., Brock, M. E., & Hume, K. (2010). Supporting implementation practices for evidence-based programs in education and special education. *Exceptional Children, 76*(4), 478–495.

Proctor, E., Silmere, H., Raghavan, R., Hovmand, P., Aarons, G., Bunger, A., Griffey, E., & Hensley, M. (2011). Outcomes for implementation research: Conceptual distinctions, measurement challenges, and research agenda. *Administration and Policy in Mental Health and Mental Health Services Research, 38*(2), 65–76.

Scheirer, M. A., & Dearing, J. W. (2011). An agenda for research on the sustainability of public health programs. *American Journal of Public Health, 101*(11), 2059–2067.

CHAPTER ELEVEN

Engaging Stakeholders

Successful educational initiatives are seldom the product of isolated efforts. Instead, they thrive on the active participation and support of a wide range of stakeholders, including parents, community members, business leaders, and external organizations. Stakeholder engagement is not just about gaining approval but about forming partnerships that enhance educational programs' relevance, effectiveness, and sustainability. This chapter explores strategies for effective stakeholder engagement, emphasizing the importance of building meaningful partnerships that drive collaborative success and promote enduring improvements in education.

Broadening Support and Resources

One of the most immediate benefits of engaging stakeholders is the expansion of resources—whether in the form of funding, expertise, or in-kind support—that become available to school districts. When districts actively involve stakeholders, they tap into a broader network of support that can enhance the scale and impact of their initiatives.

"Engaging stakeholders effectively broadens the support base, making diverse resources available for educational initiatives" (Bryk et al., 2010). For example, local businesses may provide financial sponsorship for after-school programs, while community organizations may offer expertise or volunteers to support student learning.

Moreover, stakeholders often bring innovative solutions to the table, offering ideas that the district may not have considered. In this way, engagement serves as a catalyst for creativity and problem-solving, ensuring that educational initiatives are well supported and effectively implemented.

Building Buy-In and Ownership

Stakeholder engagement is not just about gathering input; it is also about building a sense of ownership and shared responsibility for the intervention's success. When stakeholders are actively involved in the decision-making process, they are more likely to feel invested in the outcome and to support the implementation efforts. This can lead to greater commitment from teachers, increased support from parents, and a more positive reception from students.

Effective stakeholder engagement involves regular communication, collaboration opportunities, and transparency in decision-making. Schools should create spaces for stakeholders to voice their concerns, ask questions, and contribute ideas throughout the implementation process. This approach improves the likelihood of successful implementation and strengthens the relationships between the school and its community.

The following figure shows an administrator's attempt to communicate key academic school functions and events to families and other stakeholders. Each year, large magnets were created and sent home with students to inform and communicate the importance of academic initiatives. The chronically underperforming high school had a distinct focus on sporting events and social engagements, yet its strategic plan highlighted the needs of academics first. This was one example of focusing entirely on implementation efforts and communicating those throughout the year through the "school/community walkthrough."

Enhancing Program Relevance and Effectiveness

Stakeholders bring a wealth of knowledge and experience to the planning and implementation phases of educational initiatives. By involving them early in the process, districts can ensure that their programs are aligned with the needs and aspirations of the community they serve.

"Programs that reflect the community's needs and aspirations are more likely to be effective and embraced" (Sanders, 2018, p. 32). For instance, when parents and community members are included

High School Parental Academic Monitoring Checklist 2022-2023☑

September	October	November	December	January
☑ Received academic monitoring checklist ☐ Reviewed my child's academic schedule for the year ☐ I have received a school calendar of events for the year ☐ Visited the school's website Filled-out and returned my child's... ☐ Emergency contact information form ☐ Lunch application ☐ Bus pass application if applicable ☐ Media release form ☐ Reviewed the district-wide code of conduct with my child ☐ Attend Open House/ Report Out Night ☐ My child has scheduled an appointment and met with their guidance counselor for a credit audit to ensure that they are on pace to graduate ☐ I have received a copy of my child's credit audit ☐ I have scheduled an appointment with the guidance department ☐ My child has signed-up for at least one after school activity ☐ I have contacted the PTO president to express interest in joining the school's Parent Teacher Organization (PTO) ☐ **Attended the School-Community Walkthrough**	☐ Received my child's first quarter progress report **10/3-10/7** ☐ Reviewed my child's academic progress (grades, attendance, and lateness to school) *If your child has received a U or Unsatisfactory on their progress report please make an appointment with their teacher(s) or guidance counselor ***October 1st-SAT test 12th graders** ***October 2nd-18th NECAP testing for 11th graders-English/Math** ***October 12th-PSATs Grades 10/11** Helpful Reminder I have prepared my child to take this important test by making sure they get plenty of rest the night before and that they arrive to school on-time. ☐ **Attended the School-Community Walkthrough**	☐ 1st quarter ends and 2nd quarter begins ☐ Received copy of 1st quarter grades ☐ I Reviewed my child's 1st quarter (grades, attendance, lateness, and teacher's comments) ☐ If necessary contact the school to schedule an appointment with your child's teacher(s) ☐ I checked my child's attendance/ lateness to school for 1st quarter ☐ I contacted Ms. Guidance with questions regarding **attendance** ☐ I contacted Mr. Principal with questions regarding **lateness** to school ☐ **11/9 & 11/10 Parent teacher conferences** ☐ **Attended the School-Community Walkthrough**	☐ I attended the 1st academic celebration & parent/ teacher conference night event *If your child has made High Honors, Honors, or Honorable Mention they will receive a congratulatory letter from the principal inviting you and your child to this special school event ☐ Received 2nd quarter progress report ☐ Reviewed my child's academic progress (grades, attendance, and lateness to school) *If your child has received a U or Unsatisfactory on their progress report please make an appointment with their teacher(s) or guidance counselor ☐ **Attended the School-Community Walkthrough**	☐ 2nd quarter ends and 3rd quarter begins ☐ I have had a mid-year conversation with my child regarding their academic progress, attandance, and lateness ☐ **Attended the School-Community Walkthrough**

Contact Your Child's School Anytime...

Rhode Island High School
15 Anywhere Here
Providence, RI 02907
401 456-9999 (Main Office)

Administrators
LIST ALL ADMINISTRATORS
Main Office Secretaries
(principal's secretary)
Guidance
LIST ALL GUIDANCE

Figure 11.1. Checklist

Carlson, J. (2004). *High School Parental Academic Monitoring Checklist.* Developed during tenure as principal at Central High School, Providence, RI.

in discussions about curriculum development, districts can design culturally relevant programs and address the specific challenges students face.

This alignment between programs and community expectations increases the likelihood of success, as stakeholders who feel invested in the outcomes are more likely to support and advocate for the initiatives actively.

Identifying Key Stakeholders

The first step in effective stakeholder engagement is identifying the individuals, groups, and organizations with a vested interest in the school/district's success. This includes parents, teachers, local businesses, nonprofits, community organizations, and educational institutions.

- **Comprehensive Identification Process:** A thorough identification process ensures no key stakeholder group is overlooked. "Identifying the right stakeholders is the first step in building a foundation for effective collaboration" (Freeman, 2015, p. 72). For example, a district embarking on a new STEM initiative may identify local technology companies, universities, and industry professionals as potential partners who can provide resources and expertise to enhance the program.

By casting a wide net in identifying stakeholders, districts can ensure that they engage a diverse and representative group that reflects the broader community.

Building Relationships

Once key stakeholders have been identified, the next step is building relationships based on trust, transparency, and mutual respect. Effective communication is central to this process, as stakeholders need to feel informed and valued.

- **Personalized Communication:** Tailor communication strategies to address different stakeholder groups' specific interests and concerns. Regular updates and transparent information sharing foster trust and openness, ensuring stakeholders feel engaged. "Effective communication is crucial for building and maintaining trust with stakeholders" (Kouzes & Posner, 2012).

For example, districts might send targeted newsletters to parents about student performance, while business leaders might receive information on partnership opportunities and potential benefits. Districts can build stronger, more personalized relationships with stakeholders by customizing communication.

Inclusive Participation

True stakeholder engagement involves more than just informing stakeholders; it requires their active participation in decision-making processes. When stakeholders are involved in shaping educational programs, they are more likely to be committed to their success.

- **Decision-Making Involvement:** Include stakeholders in decision-making through committees, focus groups, and advisory boards. "Involving stakeholders in decision-making processes increases their commitment and enhances the relevancy of decisions" (Hart, 1992). For instance, districts might form parent advisory boards to provide input on school policies or convene focus groups of local business leaders to discuss workforce readiness programs.

This level of involvement fosters a sense of ownership among stakeholders, who feel that their voices are being heard and have a meaningful role in shaping the future of education in their community.

Partnership Development

Creating partnerships requires more than just informal agreements; it often benefits from formal structures that clarify roles, expectations, and contributions. Formal agreements help solidify the partnership and ensure that both parties clearly understand the mutual benefits and responsibilities.

- **Formal Agreements:** Where appropriate, formalize partnerships through agreements or memorandums of understanding (MOUs) that outline the terms of the collaboration. "Formal agreements help in defining the terms and expectations of partnerships, making them more effective" (Senge, 2006). For example, an MOU between a school district and a local community college might detail how both institutions will collaborate to offer dual-enrollment courses for high school students.

These agreements provide a clear framework for collaboration and help ensure that partnerships remain strong and sustainable over time.

Mutual Benefits

For partnerships to thrive, all parties involved must see tangible benefits from the relationship. When partners perceive that their contributions are valued and that they are gaining something in return, they are likelier to remain engaged and committed.

- **Identifying and Communicating Benefits:** Clearly articulate the benefits of the partnership for all involved parties. "Win-win is about constantly seeking mutual benefit in all human interactions—about finding solutions that are truly beneficial and satisfying for everyone involved" (Covey, 1989, p. 207). For example, local businesses may benefit from enhanced brand visibility and the opportunity to contribute to workforce development initiatives. In contrast, schools benefit from the resources and expertise these partners provide.

By ensuring that partnerships are mutually beneficial, districts can build stronger, more sustainable relationships that contribute to long-term educational success.

Community Engagement Events

In addition to formal agreements and communication, districts can foster stakeholder engagement through community events that bring people together to discuss educational priorities and collaborate on initiatives.

- **Workshops and Forums:** Organize workshops, forums, and public meetings that allow stakeholders to interact directly with the district and each other. "Engagement events are vital platforms for dialogue, feedback, and community involvement" (Putnam, 2000). These events allow stakeholders to voice their opinions, offer suggestions, and stay informed about the district's activities.

For example, a district might host a community forum to discuss a new school construction project, inviting parents, local government officials, and business leaders to share their perspectives and concerns. These events help build community cohesion and ensure all voices are considered in decision-making.

Feedback Mechanisms

To continuously improve stakeholder engagement efforts, districts need to collect regular feedback from stakeholders to assess the effectiveness of their strategies.

- **Surveys and Feedback Forms:** Implement tools such as surveys and feedback forms to gather input from stakeholders about their satisfaction and the perceived effectiveness of engagement efforts. "Regular feedback helps in continuously improving engagement strategies" (Dufour & Marzano, 2011, p. 92). For instance, after hosting a community event, districts might send out surveys to participants asking for feedback on what went well and what could be improved.

This feedback can provide valuable insights into how districts can refine their engagement efforts and better meet the needs of their stakeholders.

Continuous Improvement

Engagement strategies should be dynamic and adaptable, evolving in response to changing needs and contexts. By remaining flexible and open to adjustment, districts can ensure that their engagement efforts remain relevant and effective over time.

- **Adjustment of Strategies:** Use stakeholder feedback to make necessary adjustments in engagement strategies. "Adaptability is key in maintaining effective stakeholder engagement over time" (Fullan, 2007). For example, if feedback reveals that certain stakeholder groups feel underrepresented in district decision-making, districts might implement new initiatives to increase participation.

Continuous improvement efforts help districts stay responsive to their communities and maintain strong, supportive relationships with stakeholders.

Conclusion

Engaging stakeholders effectively is essential for the success and sustainability of educational initiatives. School districts can ensure that the broader community supports and enriches their educational efforts by identifying key stakeholders, building strong relationships, creating mutually beneficial partnerships, and continuously evaluating and adapting engagement strategies. These partnerships bring additional resources and perspectives and foster a shared commitment to student success and educational excellence.

Questions for Reflection

To deepen your understanding of stakeholder engagement and its role in educational success, consider the following questions:

1. How can districts ensure that they are identifying and engaging the right stakeholders for their educational initiatives?
2. Why is it important for stakeholders to be involved in decision-making processes, and how can districts create opportunities for meaningful stakeholder participation?

3. What role do formal agreements play in sustaining partnerships, and how can districts ensure that partnerships are mutually beneficial?
4. How can community engagement events foster stronger relationships between districts and their stakeholders, and what strategies can districts use to maximize the impact of these events?
5. What strategies can districts use to continuously evaluate and improve their stakeholder engagement efforts, ensuring that they remain effective over time?

Bibliography

Bryk, A. S., Sebring, P. B., Allensworth, E., Luppescu, S., & Easton, J. Q. (2010). *Organizing schools for improvement: Lessons from Chicago*. University of Chicago Press.

Covey, S. R. (1989). *The 7 habits of highly effective people: Powerful lessons in personal change*. Free Press.

DuFour, R., & Marzano, R. J. (2011). *Leaders of learning: How district, school, and classroom leaders improve student achievement*. Solution Tree Press.

Freeman, R. E. (2015). *Strategic management: A stakeholder approach*. Cambridge University Press.

Fullan, M. (2007). *The new meaning of educational change*. Teachers College Press.

Hart, R. (1992). *Children's participation: From tokenism to citizenship*. UNICEF International Child Development Centre.

Kouzes, J. M., & Posner, B. Z. (2012). *The leadership challenge: How to make extraordinary things happen in organizations*. Jossey-Bass.

Putnam, R. D. (2000). *Bowling alone: The collapse and revival of American community*. Simon & Schuster.

Sanders, M. G. (2018). *Schooling students placed at risk: Research, policy, and practice in the education of poor and minority adolescents*. Lawrence Erlbaum Associates.

Senge, P. M. (2006). *The fifth discipline: The art and practice of the learning organization*. Doubleday.

CHAPTER TWELVE

Celebrating Success and Sustaining Momentum

Effective educational leadership goes beyond the mere planning and implementation of improvement strategies. It involves recognizing and celebrating successes essential to maintaining morale, reinforcing the value of initiatives, and embedding successful practices into the school district's culture. Celebrating milestones and achievements boosts motivation and momentum, ensuring positive changes endure over time. This chapter explores how districts can recognize achievements, celebrate key milestones, and integrate successful practices into their educational culture to sustain progress and foster excellence.

Motivation and Morale

Celebrating success serves as a powerful motivator for both educators and students. Recognition of hard work and dedication boosts morale, leading to sustained effort and a more substantial commitment to excellence. When individuals feel their contributions are valued, they are more likely to remain engaged and motivated.

"Recognition and celebration are powerful motivators that enhance team spirit and personal commitment" (Kouzes & Posner, 2012, p. 99). By regularly acknowledging achievements, districts can foster a positive environment where students and educators are inspired to continue pushing toward tremendous success.

For example, a district that publicly recognizes the efforts of teachers who have significantly improved student literacy rates not only boosts those teachers' morale but also inspires others to adopt similar practices and aim for similar achievements.

Validation and Support

Celebrations validate the efforts of all stakeholders, from teachers and students to administrators and community partners. By highlighting the positive outcomes of educational initiatives, districts can build broader community support and demonstrate the tangible benefits of their efforts.

"Celebrating successes provides tangible evidence that the effort is worthwhile and encourages community support and involvement" (Pink, 2009). When communities see the impact of their contributions—whether through improved student outcomes or successful programs—they are more likely to remain engaged and continue offering financial, volunteer, or advisory support.

Celebrations also allow districts to communicate the value of their initiatives within the school and the broader community, showcasing the importance of sustained investment in education.

Formal Recognition Programs

One effective way to celebrate success is through formal recognition programs. These programs institutionalize celebrating achievements and ensure that accomplishments are acknowledged meaningfully and consistently.

- **Implementing Formal Recognition Programs:** Districts can establish regular awards ceremonies, create public commendations, or feature successful individuals and teams in district-wide publications. "Formal recognition programs help institutionalize the practice of celebrating success" (Senge, 2006). For example, an annual teacher excellence award ceremony could highlight outstanding teaching practices, providing a platform for sharing success stories and best practices across the district.

By formalizing the recognition process, districts ensure that success is celebrated consistently, fostering a culture that values and rewards excellence.

Incorporate Recognition into Everyday Practices

While formal recognition is essential, districts should integrate recognition into daily or weekly routines to ensure that achievements are acknowledged continuously.

- **Embedding Recognition into Daily Practices:** Regular shout-outs in staff meetings, features in school newsletters, or moments of praise during professional gatherings help maintain high morale and reinforce the importance of continuous achievement. "Integrating recognition into regular practices ensures that achievements are consistently celebrated, keeping morale high" (Gostick & Elton, 2009, p. 30).

For instance, a principal might highlight a teacher's innovative lesson plan during a staff meeting or send a district-wide email celebrating a school's improved test scores. These everyday moments of recognition create a culture where success is appreciated and celebrated frequently.

Event Celebrations

Celebrating critical milestones in school projects or initiatives through organized events is another way to acknowledge success and build momentum. These events allow stakeholders to witness the impact of their efforts firsthand and share in the joy of achievement.

- **Organizing Event Celebrations:** Open houses, exhibitions, presentations, and other celebratory events allow schools to showcase progress and achievements. "Events provide a platform for the community to come together and celebrate achievements, which boosts visibility and support for school initiatives" (Heath & Heath, 2010, p. 203). For example, a school might host an exhibition showcasing student projects from a new science curriculum, inviting parents and community members to celebrate the students' work.

These events help create a sense of community pride and demonstrate the value of the district's efforts, further solidifying support for ongoing initiatives.

Community Involvement

Involving the community in celebrations is key to enhancing the impact of these events and strengthening the relationship between the school and the wider community.

- **Encouraging Community Involvement:** Districts can invite families, local businesses, and media to participate in or sponsor celebratory events. "Community involvement in celebrations enhances the event's impact and strengthens community-school relationships" (Putnam, 2000, p. 57). For instance, a district could invite local businesses to sponsor awards for student achievement, encourage parents to attend recognition ceremonies, or conduct school/community walkthroughs so individuals can see how classrooms run.

By fostering strong community ties, districts ensure that their initiatives are supported by a broad base of stakeholders who are invested in the school system's long-term success.

Policy and Practice Integration

To sustain successful practices over time, districts must embed these strategies into the policies and daily operations of the school. This ensures that improvements become permanent features of the school culture rather than temporary fixes.

- **Integrating Success into Policies and Practices:** Districts should work to codify successful strategies into their policies and procedures, ensuring that these practices are followed consistently. "Embedding successful practices into policies and daily routines helps transform these practices into enduring features of the school culture" (Fullan, 2007). For example, if a particular instructional strategy has proven effective in raising test scores, it should be incorporated into the district's curriculum guidelines and professional development programs.

When successful practices are integrated into the district's daily operations, they become standard operating procedures, helping to sustain positive outcomes over the long term.

Professional Development

Ongoing professional development is critical for reinforcing and expanding upon successful strategies. Continuous training ensures that educators remain up to date on best practices and are equipped to implement successful strategies effectively.

- **Offering Professional Development:** Districts should offer regular professional development opportunities that align with successful strategies. "Ongoing professional development ensures that all educators understand, adopt, and refine successful practices" (Darling-Hammond, 2010, p. 52). For example, a district might offer workshops on differentiated instruction to reinforce successful methods that have improved student engagement and performance.

Districts can ensure that successful practices continue to evolve and improve over time by providing teachers and staff with opportunities to learn and grow.

Leadership Support

Strong leadership is essential for maintaining focus and momentum. School leaders are crucial in championing successful practices, reinforcing their importance, and prioritizing celebrations and recognition.

- **Ensuring Leadership Commitment:** School leadership must continuously support and promote successful practices, ensuring they remain central to the district's operations. "Whenever you let up before the job is done, critical momentum can be lost and regression may follow" (Kotter, 1996, p. 133). This underscores the necessity of leadership commitment in sustaining change efforts and embedding new practices within an organization's culture.

When leaders are visibly engaged in celebrating successes and advocating for the continued implementation of successful strategies, it reinforces the importance of these efforts. It encourages ongoing dedication from the entire school community.

Conclusion

Celebrating success and embedding effective practices into the school district's culture is crucial for the long-term sustainability of school improvement efforts. By recognizing achievements, celebrating milestones, and ensuring successful strategies become a permanent part of the school culture, districts can enhance morale, build community support, and lay a strong foundation for future successes. These efforts help sustain momentum, ensuring that progress is maintained and continuously built upon, advancing educational excellence for all students.

Questions for Reflection

To deepen your understanding of how to celebrate success and sustain momentum in educational initiatives, consider the following questions:

1. How can districts create formal recognition programs that consistently celebrate both individual and team achievements?
2. What are the benefits of embedding recognition into daily practices, and how can districts implement this effectively?
3. How can community involvement in celebratory events strengthen relationships between schools and their surrounding communities?

4. Why is it important to embed successful practices into school policies and daily routines, and how can districts ensure that these practices are sustained over time?
5. What role does continuous leadership support play in sustaining momentum, and how can leaders maintain focus on celebrating success and embedding successful practices?

Bibliography

Darling-Hammond, L. (2010). *The flat world and education: How America's commitment to equity will determine our future.* Teachers College Press.

Fullan, M. (2007). *The new meaning of educational change.* Teachers College Press.

Gostick, A., & Elton, C. (2009). *The carrot principle: How the best managers use recognition to engage their people, retain talent, and accelerate performance.* Free Press.

Heath, C., & Heath, D. (2010). *Switch: How to change things when change is hard.* Broadway Books.

Kotter, J. P. (1996). *Leading change.* Harvard Business Review Press.

Kouzes, J. M., & Posner, B. Z. (2012). *The leadership challenge: How to make extraordinary things happen in organizations.* Jossey-Bass.

Pink, D. H. (2009). *Drive: The surprising truth about what motivates us.* Riverhead Books.

Putnam, R. D. (2000). *Bowling alone: The collapse and revival of American community.* Simon & Schuster.

Senge, P. M. (2006). *The fifth discipline: The art and practice of the learning organization.* Doubleday.

CHAPTER THIRTEEN

Case Studies

Effectively using data and community engagement in school districts can drive significant educational improvements, optimize resource allocation, and foster partnerships that support student achievement. Through case studies and examples, this chapter illustrates how districts nationwide have successfully leveraged data dashboards, community partnerships, and innovative programs to enhance educational outcomes. By exploring these real-world scenarios, academic leaders can draw valuable lessons to apply in their districts, fostering continuous improvement and building stronger connections with their communities.

Case Studies and Examples

Example 1: A District Using Data Dashboards

Leaders in a suburban school district recognized the need for a more efficient way to monitor student performance and engagement. To address this, the district implemented a data dashboard that provides real-time insights into key performance metrics, including attendance, grades, and behavioral data. This tool has enabled administrators and educators to quickly identify issues such as attendance drops or decreases in academic performance, allowing for timely interventions.

"Data dashboards provide immediate insights that are crucial for timely interventions" (Specht, n.d.). The dashboard has empowered educators to be more proactive in their approaches, as they can now monitor trends and respond before issues escalate. For example, when a student's attendance declines, the system flags the problem, enabling school staff to contact the family and provide support. Similarly, if a student's grades begin to drop, the dashboard prompts early intervention strategies, such as tutoring or personalized learning plans.

Example 2: Community-Engaged Review Process

Leaders in an urban school district sought to involve the community more deeply in evaluating and shaping educational programs. The district established a community-engaged review process that includes parents, local businesses, and nonprofit organizations in the assessment and planning phases. This inclusive approach has resulted in programs that are more closely aligned with community needs, thereby increasing public support and relevance.

"Engaging community members as active partners in the evaluation process enhances the relevance and effectiveness of educational programs" (Belone et al., 2016). For instance, one of the outcomes of this process was the introduction of after-school tutoring programs explicitly tailored to the needs of students from economically disadvantaged backgrounds. These programs were co-designed with input from local organizations that understood the community's challenges, leading to higher participation rates and improved student performance.

Example 3: Rural District Resource Optimization

A rural school district faced budget constraints and needed to find ways to optimize its resources without sacrificing student services. District leaders turned to data to analyze school bus routes, student demographic information, and transportation costs. By using these data, the district was able to redesign its bus routes, resulting in substantial cost savings that were redirected toward student learning resources, such as new technology and instructional materials.

"Optimizing operations based on data can free up resources for direct educational purposes" (Specht, n.d.). The district's ability to optimize its transportation system not only saved money but also improved the overall efficiency of its operations, allowing more funds to be allocated directly to classroom instruction and student support.

Example 4: Innovative Practice Workshops

Another district hosts quarterly workshops, during which teachers share successful instructional strategies and innovations with their peers. These workshops are designed to facilitate the dissemination of best practices and ensure that effective teaching methods are implemented consistently across the district.

In the Learning Policy Institute's report titled "Effective Teacher Professional Development," the authors highlight that effective professional development "supports collaboration: High-quality professional development creates space for teachers to share ideas and collaborate in their learning, often in job-embedded contexts" (Darling-Hammond et al., 2017). This collaborative approach enables educators to build communities that positively influence the culture and instruction across various levels, including grade levels, departments, schools, and districts.

Conclusion

The case studies and examples presented in this chapter illustrate the diverse ways in which school districts can use data and community engagement to drive educational success. Whether through data dashboards, community partnerships, or innovative programs, these districts have demonstrated that a proactive, data-informed approach can improve student outcomes. By celebrating achievements, engaging stakeholders, and embedding successful practices into district culture, these districts have sustained momentum and created environments where excellence thrives.

Questions for Reflection

To further your understanding of how data and community engagement can drive educational success, consider the following questions:

1. How can districts effectively implement data dashboards to improve real-time decision-making and interventions?
2. What are the benefits of engaging the community in reviewing and evaluating educational programs, and how can districts build strong community partnerships?

3. How can districts use data to identify areas for improvement and implement targeted interventions that lead to significant performance gains?
4. What strategies can districts use to enhance parent involvement and community engagement to support student achievement?
5. How do district-wide celebrations and workshops contribute to a district's overall culture, and what steps can districts take to ensure that these events foster continuous improvement and success?

Bibliography

Belone, L., Lucero, J. E., Duran, B., Tafoya, G., Baker, E. A., Chan, D., Chang, C., Greene-Moton, E., Kelley, M., & Wallerstein, N. (2016). Community-Engaged Pedagogy: A Strengths-Based Approach to Involving Diverse Stakeholders in Research Partnerships. *Progress in Community Health Partnerships: Research, Education, and Action, 10*(1), 19–29.

Darling-Hammond, L., Hyler, M. E., & Gardner, M. (2017). Effective teacher professional development (Fact Sheet). Learning Policy Institute.

Specht, D. (n.d.). How administrators are using data dashboards to improve decision-making. Otus. https://otus.com/blog/how-administrators-are-using-data-dashboards-to-improve-decision-making/

PART V

Effective Implementation

Effective implementation of Implementation Science (IS) is critical in transforming evidence-based practices into meaningful, sustainable educational improvements. Implementation Science provides a structured approach for educators, administrators, and policymakers to bridge the gap between research and real-world application, ensuring that programs with proven effectiveness are applied to meet the unique needs of diverse educational contexts. The framework of Implementation Science emphasizes not only the fidelity to core components of an intervention but also the adaptability necessary for addressing varying student populations, school environments, and resource capacities.

Effective implementation is essential in the context of literacy and the Science of Reading (SoR). Research-driven reading interventions—focusing on key components such as phonemic awareness, phonics, vocabulary, and comprehension—hold the potential to significantly enhance literacy outcomes. However, the success of these interventions depends on how accurately and consistently they are applied. When implemented effectively, Implementation Science practices ensure that educators are equipped with the skills, support, and resources needed to deliver SoR interventions with precision and adaptability.

Without effective implementation, even the most well-researched interventions may fall short, leading to inconsistencies in student outcomes and lost opportunities for literacy advancement. Therefore, understanding and applying the principles of Implementation Science in literacy education is essential for achieving and sustaining high-quality, equitable reading instruction across schools and districts. This chapter delves into the core components and challenges of implementing SoR interventions effectively, illustrating the power of Implementation Science in driving positive, lasting change in literacy education.

Implementation Science tackles a pressing challenge in education: ensuring that interventions that show proven effectiveness in controlled research settings can be successfully applied and sustained in diverse educational environments. Effective implementation is critical in SoR, where research-based practices need to be carried out with fidelity to improve reading outcomes, especially for students who struggle with literacy.

Balancing Fidelity and Flexibility in SoR Implementation

A central challenge in SoR implementation is achieving the right balance between maintaining fidelity to evidence-based instructional components—such as phonemic awareness, phonics, fluency, vocabulary, and comprehension—and allowing for the flexibility needed to adapt instruction to specific classroom contexts. Fidelity ensures that the intervention retains the core elements that contribute to its success, while flexibility permits adaptations that meet the unique needs of students and schools.

For example, the Orton-Gillingham (OG) approach, a structured, multisensory phonics-based reading intervention, has shown strong positive outcomes for students with dyslexia when implemented with fidelity. Research indicates that OG, when implemented consistently and with adherence to its core instructional practices, can lead to significant gains in reading accuracy and fluency (Torgesen, 2000). However, educators in diverse settings might adapt the pacing or incorporate culturally relevant materials to engage their students better, exemplifying a balance of fidelity and flexibility (Kilpatrick, 2015).

Importance of Ongoing Training and Support

A pillar of effective SoR implementation is ongoing training and support for educators. Teachers need a solid understanding of the components of SoR to implement interventions effectively, which includes initial training and continuous professional development.

Studies underscore that professional development and in-class coaching greatly enhance teachers' ability to apply SoR principles accurately. For instance, the LETRS (Language Essentials for Teachers of Reading and Spelling) program, designed by Louisa Moats, provides teachers with foundational knowledge of SoR and has led to improvements in literacy instruction quality and student reading achievement when coupled with coaching support (Moats & Tolman, 2019). Schools implementing LETRS provide teachers with training sessions, regular observations, and feedback, fostering an environment where teachers can adapt SoR practices to best support students while maintaining instructional integrity.

Leveraging Technology to Enhance SoR Interventions

Technology has become increasingly significant in implementing and sustaining SoR interventions. Advanced technologies such as artificial intelligence (AI) and data analytics support iterative assessment and adaptation of SoR programs in real time, making it possible for educators to tailor instruction based on student needs more efficiently.

An example of this is Amplify's mCLASS with DIBELS 8th Edition, an AI-driven assessment tool that identifies reading difficulties early, tracks progress, and suggests instructional modifications. This tool supports the sustainability of SoR interventions by providing real-time data on student performance, allowing teachers to adjust their instruction accordingly. Studies reveal that frequent formative assessments, like those in mCLASS, can lead to significant gains in reading fluency and comprehension when combined with appropriate instructional responses (Good & Kaminski, 2021).

Overcoming Common Challenges in SoR Implementation

While IS offers a framework for successful educational improvement, schools encounter challenges such as time constraints, limited resources, and the need for continuous evaluation.

One challenge in SoR implementation is the time required for teachers to internalize and deliver evidence-based literacy practices, as well as the resources needed for high-quality materials and assessments. Strategic planning, realistic goal setting, and leadership commitment are essential to overcoming these limitations.

For instance, in Mississippi's state-wide literacy initiative, a phased implementation approach was employed to train teachers in the SoR over several years, focusing on building capacity at each stage. The initiative included targeted coaching and funding for resources, leading to a significant increase in reading proficiency scores across the state (The Nation's Report Card, 2022). This example highlights the importance of adequate investment in training and support, as well as the gradual scaling of interventions for sustainability.

Embracing Continuous Adaptation and Evaluation

Educational environments are dynamic, and SoR interventions must be continuously evaluated and adapted to meet students' needs effectively. Schools and districts committed to ongoing data collection and analysis can make informed instructional adjustments based on student progress.

For example, Arkansas's Reading Initiative for Student Excellence (RISE) implements iterative evaluation by training educators to use data effectively and adjust based on assessment results. RISE focuses on data-driven instruction, leading to significant improvements in early literacy outcomes across the state (Smith, 2021).

Scaling and Sustaining SoR Interventions

Scaling SoR interventions from classrooms to entire districts and sustaining them over time demands a strategic approach. Strong leadership at both school and district levels is essential, along with clear goals, success benchmarks, and systems for tracking progress.

An illustrative example is Tennessee's Early Literacy Network, where district and state leaders worked collaboratively to support the implementation of SoR practices across multiple schools. The initiative provided funding, training, and technical support to sustain the intervention, contributing to statewide gains in early literacy scores over successive years (Tennessee Department of Education, 2022). This example highlights how leadership, strategic planning, and sustained support drive successful scaling and the sustainability of evidence-based reading interventions.

Implementation Science offers a powerful framework for applying SoR principles effectively across varied educational contexts. Schools can achieve meaningful and sustainable improvements in reading outcomes by maintaining a balance between fidelity and flexibility, providing ongoing training and support, leveraging technology, and addressing challenges like time constraints and resource limitations. When applied thoughtfully, these principles ensure that the benefits of SoR are accessible to all students, creating a foundation for lifelong literacy and academic success.

Questions for Reflection

To deepen your understanding of Implementation Science in education and its role in driving school improvement, consider the following questions:

1. How can educators and school leaders balance the need for fidelity to core Science of Reading (SoR) principles with the flexibility required to address diverse classroom contexts and student needs?
2. What role does ongoing professional development and coaching play in ensuring the effective implementation of SoR practices, and how can schools sustain this support over time?
3. In what ways can technology, such as AI-driven assessment tools, enhance the effectiveness and sustainability of SoR interventions? What potential challenges might arise in relying on technology for literacy improvement?
4. What strategies can schools and districts employ to overcome common challenges—such as time constraints, limited resources, and the need for continuous adaptation—during the implementation of SoR interventions?

5. How can educational leaders effectively monitor and evaluate SoR interventions over time to ensure that they meet evolving student needs and contribute to long-term literacy gains?
6. What critical factors should be considered when scaling SoR interventions from a single classroom to an entire district to ensure successful and sustainable outcomes for all students?

Bibliography

Good, R. H., & Kaminski, R. A. (2021). *Dynamic Indicators of Basic Early Literacy Skills (DIBELS).* University of Oregon.

Kilpatrick, D. A. (2015). *Essentials of assessing, preventing, and overcoming reading difficulties.* John Wiley & Sons.

Moats, L. C., & Tolman, C. (2019). *LETRS (Language Essentials for Teachers of Reading and Spelling) Modules.* Voyager Sopris Learning.

Smith, J. (2021). *Arkansas's Reading Initiative for Student Excellence (RISE) evaluation report.* https://dese.ade.arkansas.gov/Offices/learning-services/rise-arkansas

Tennessee Department of Education. (2022). *Early Literacy Network Impact Report.* https://comptroller.tn.gov/content/dam/cot/orea/advanced-search/2022/Literacy.pdf

Torgesen, J. K. (2000). Individual differences in response to early interventions in reading. *Learning Disabilities Research & Practice, 15*(1), 55–64.

The Nation's Report Card. (2022). *Mississippi's literacy initiative outcomes.* https://nces.ed.gov/nationsreportcard/subject/publications/stt2022/pdf/2023010MS4.pdf

CHAPTER FOURTEEN

Selecting Evidence-Based Practices

Implementation Science is dedicated to bridging the gap between research to practice, ensuring that evidence-based interventions are effectively adopted and sustained in real-world settings. Successful implementation relies on a series of components that guide the process, from selecting appropriate strategies to monitoring outcomes and ensuring long-term sustainability. This chapter explores key components of Implementation Science—implementation strategies, outcomes, and sustainability—and provides real-world examples of how these elements come together in schools and districts.

High-Quality Instructional Material Review

The selection of a new early literacy curriculum is a critical decision that requires careful evaluation to ensure it aligns with the needs of students and supports effective teaching practices. The high-quality instructional material (HQIM) review provides a rigorous framework for districts to make informed decisions, ensuring the chosen materials foster foundational literacy skills, such as phonemic awareness, phonics, fluency, vocabulary, and comprehension, that are crucial for early literacy development (Kilpatrick, 2015). A HQIM review process serves as a structured approach to assess potential curricula based on a range of criteria, such as alignment with state and national standards, evidence of effectiveness, and adaptability to diverse learners.

The HQIM review typically begins with the formation of a curriculum review committee composed of educators, literacy specialists, and administrators but, dependent on a district size, it may be the same team that conducted the strategic planning. This committee's role is to evaluate several curriculum options through a multiphase process. First, they assess whether each curriculum aligns with research-based best practices, particularly those grounded in the Science of Reading, which emphasizes systematic, explicit instruction in early literacy skills (Moats, 2020). The committee also evaluates the content's rigor and its ability to meet the needs of diverse student populations, including English Language Learners (ELLs) and students with learning disabilities, ensuring that the curriculum provides adequate support for differentiated instruction.

In addition to content alignment, the review process considers the usability of the materials. Pilot programs are often employed, allowing teachers to try the curriculum in their classrooms and provide feedback on how well it integrates with current instructional practices. For example, teachers in the Fall River Public Schools piloted several early literacy programs as part of an HQIM review, gathering data on student engagement, ease of implementation, and teacher support resources. Teachers reported on how well the materials helped them address learning gaps, particularly in schools with high percentages of struggling readers. This hands-on approach gave the review committee valuable insights into the practicality and effectiveness of the curricula being considered.

Ultimately, the HQIM review ensures that the selected early literacy curriculum not only meets academic standards but also provides teachers with the necessary resources and support to implement the program effectively. By involving educators in the decision-making process, the review encourages teacher buy-in and helps to ensure the new curriculum is embraced and implemented with fidelity across the district. This rigorous, collaborative approach promotes the selection of a curriculum that will support long-term literacy success for all students.

Selection and Tailoring

The success of an intervention depends on selecting and tailoring implementation strategies to fit the specific context of the school or district. Each educational setting has unique characteristics—student demographics, available resources, and organizational culture—that affect how an intervention is received and implemented. Therefore a one-size-fits-all approach is rarely practical. Tailoring strategies to address the specific needs, barriers, and facilitators in a particular context increases the likelihood of success.

"Tailored implementation strategies are more likely to be effective as they address the specific barriers and facilitators in a given context" (Powell et al., 2015, p. 177). For example, in a district with limited funding for professional development, the selection of implementation strategies might prioritize cost-effective online training for teachers, coupled with local coaching support. In another context, where teachers may resist adopting new technologies, strategies might include hands-on training sessions and peer-led workshops to build comfort and confidence.

The selection of high-quality instructional materials is critical to the success of any early literacy intervention. Effective implementation begins with choosing curricula and resources that are not only evidence-based but also aligned with the specific needs of the school or district. A thoughtful selection process, grounded in research and responsive to the local context, ensures that the chosen materials will support student achievement and promote long-term literacy development. Educational leaders must employ a rigorous evaluation process to assess how well instructional materials align with curriculum standards, accommodate diverse learning needs, and fit within the operational capacity of the school or district.

The process of selecting instructional materials should begin with a thorough review of available curricula, focusing on those with a proven track record of success in literacy education. This involves evaluating research and efficacy studies to ensure that the materials are supported by strong evidence, particularly for early literacy instruction, where the foundational skills of phonics, phonemic awareness, fluency, and comprehension are critical (Kilpatrick, 2015). Educational leaders must consider whether the instructional materials align with state standards and curriculum frameworks, as well as whether they address the diverse needs of students, including ELLs and students with learning disabilities.

In the context of selecting early literacy curricula, it is essential to engage stakeholders—including teachers, curriculum specialists, and instructional leaders—throughout the evaluation process. Involving educators who will use the materials in the classroom ensures that the selection process is practical and grounded in the realities of daily instruction. For example, districts often establish curriculum review committees to vet instructional materials through a multiphase evaluation process that includes a review of alignment with learning standards, analysis of content depth, and feedback from pilot implementations. This approach allows educators to test the usability and effectiveness of the materials before committing to full-scale adoption (Desimone & Garet, 2015).

Additionally, the evaluation process must consider the long-term sustainability of the instructional materials. This includes assessing whether the curriculum provides ongoing support, such as supplemental materials or digital resources, and whether it aligns with the district's capacity for teacher training and professional development. In districts where resources are limited, for instance, the evaluation might prioritize materials that include comprehensive, cost-effective online training modules, ensuring that teachers can access the support they need without overburdening the district financially (Powell et al., 2015).

The selection and evaluation of high-quality instructional materials for early literacy require a deliberate, multiphase process that incorporates stakeholder input, alignment with standards, and a focus on adaptability to diverse learning needs. By employing rigorous evaluation criteria and piloting potential curricula, districts can ensure that the materials they choose will promote student success and provide the necessary support for effective implementation.

Multifaceted Approaches

In many cases, relying on a single implementation strategy is insufficient to address the complex needs of schools and districts. Multifaceted approaches, which combine several strategies to target different aspects of the implementation process, are more effective. These approaches might include a combination of education, incentives, coaching, and feedback mechanisms to support adopting new practices.

"Multifaceted approaches that combine several strategies are often more effective than single strategies" (Powell et al., 2015, pp. 177–194). For instance, a district introducing a new behavior management system might implement a multifaceted strategy that includes initial training sessions for teachers, regular coaching from behavior specialists, feedback loops to monitor progress, and incentives for schools that demonstrate high fidelity in implementing the new system.

Implementation Outcomes

Acceptability

One key outcome of any implementation effort is acceptability—the perception among stakeholders that the intervention is agreeable, beneficial, and satisfactory. Acceptability reflects the extent to which teachers, students, administrators, and parents are willing to support and engage with the intervention. Without broad acceptability, an intervention is unlikely to be implemented effectively or sustained over time.

"Acceptability is a key outcome as it reflects the extent to which stakeholders are willing to support and engage with the intervention" (Proctor et al., 2011, p. 67). For example, a district that implements a new reading intervention must ensure that teachers find the program acceptable by addressing their concerns, providing adequate training, and demonstrating student potential benefits. When stakeholders perceive the intervention as useful and aligned with their values, they are more likely to adopt and support it.

Feasibility

Feasibility refers to the practicality of implementing an intervention within the school or district's specific constraints. This includes resource availability, staff capacity, and organizational readiness. Feasibility is important because even the most effective interventions will fail if they cannot be practically implemented within the existing infrastructure.

"Feasibility is about practicality—whether the intervention can be implemented within the existing constraints" (Proctor et al., 2011, p. 69). For example, a district considering implementing a new digital literacy program must assess whether schools have the necessary technology, internet access, and teacher capacity to support the program. If these conditions are not met, the district may need to adjust the intervention or invest additional resources to ensure feasibility.

In the San Diego Unified School District, feasibility was a key concern when the district introduced a new science curriculum that required extensive lab materials and technology. To address this, the district phased in the curriculum over several years, starting with schools with the necessary infrastructure. This phased approach allowed the district to address feasibility concerns gradually, ensuring that all schools could successfully implement the new curriculum over time.

Sustainability

Sustainability is the ultimate goal of any implementation effort. It refers to the ability of an intervention to be maintained over time and become an integral part of the school or district's operations. For an intervention to be sustainable, it must be embedded into everyday practice and supported by ongoing leadership, resources, and infrastructure.

"Sustainability is about embedding the intervention into everyday practice so that it continues to deliver benefits long after initial implementation" (Scheirer & Dearing, 2011). For example, a district that implements a new data-driven instructional approach must ensure that the necessary data systems, professional development, and leadership support are in place to sustain the approach over the long term.

Adaptability

Another key component of sustainability is adaptability—the intervention's ability to evolve in response to changing circumstances and needs. An intervention that can be adjusted without losing its core elements will likely remain relevant and effective over time. Adaptability ensures that schools and districts can continue to benefit from the intervention even as new challenges and opportunities arise.

"An intervention that can adapt to changing circumstances and needs is more likely to be sustained over time" (Moore et al., 2021). For example, a district that implements a blended learning model may need to adapt the program to changes in technology, student needs, or state policies. By allowing for flexibility and adaptation, the district can ensure that the intervention remains effective in the long run.

Conclusion

The components of Implementation Science—implementation strategies, outcomes, and sustainability—are critical for ensuring that evidence-based interventions are successfully adopted and maintained in educational settings. By selecting and tailoring strategies to fit the specific context, monitoring key outcomes such as acceptability, feasibility, and fidelity, and focusing on long-term sustainability and adaptability, schools and districts can effectively implement and sustain interventions that lead to meaningful improvements in student outcomes.

Through careful planning, monitoring, and adaptation, educational leaders can navigate the complexities of implementation, ensuring that new practices are not only adopted but also embedded into the fabric of the school or district. The framework provided by Implementation Science offers a road map for achieving successful and sustainable change in education.

Questions for Reflection

To deepen your understanding of the components of Implementation Science and their application in education, consider the following questions:

1. How do we ensure that selected evidence-based practices are closely aligned with the unique needs of our students and the goals of our district?

2. What criteria should we prioritize when reviewing high-quality instructional materials (HQIM) for early literacy programs?
3. How can we involve key stakeholders, including teachers, administrators, and families, in the selection and planning process to enhance buy-in and successful implementation?
4. What tools and methods can we use to monitor the feasibility, acceptability, and fidelity of the new curriculum during the implementation phase?
5. How can we plan for the sustainability of evidence-based practices over the long term?

Bibliography

Desimone, L. M., & Garet, M. S. (2015). Best practices in teachers' professional development in the United States. *Psychology, Society & Education, 7*(3), 252–263.

Kilpatrick, D. A. (2015). *Essentials of assessing, preventing, and overcoming reading difficulties.* Wiley.

Moats, L. C. (2020). *Teaching reading is rocket science: What expert teachers of reading should know and be able to do.* American Federation of Teachers.

Moore, G., Campbell, M., Copeland, L., Craig, P., Movsisyan, A., Hoddinott, P., Littlecott, H., O'Cathain, A., Pfadenhauer, L., Rehfuess, E., Segrott, J., Hawe, P., Kee, F., Couturiaux, D., Hallingberg, B., & Evans, R. (2021). Adapting interventions to new contexts—the ADAPT guidance. *BMJ*, 374, n1679. https://doi.org/10.1136/bmj.n1679

Powell, B. J., Beidas, R. S., Lewis, C. C., Aarons, G. A., McMillen, J. C., Proctor, E. K., & Mandell, D. S. (2015). Methods to improve the selection and tailoring of implementation strategies. *Journal of Behavioral Health Services & Research, 42*(2), 177–193.

Proctor, E., Silmere, H., Raghavan, R., Hovmand, P., Aarons, G., Bunger, A., Griffey, R., & Hensley, M. (2011). Outcomes for implementation research: Conceptual distinctions, measurement challenges, and research agenda. *Administration and Policy in Mental Health and Mental Health Services Research, 38*(2), 65–76.

Scheirer, M. A., & Dearing, J. W. (2011). An agenda for research on the sustainability of public health programs. *American Journal of Public Health, 101*(11), 2059–2067.

CHAPTER FIFTEEN

Stages of Implementation

Implementation Science provides a structured approach to ensure that evidence-based interventions are successfully integrated into practice in educational settings. The three "buckets" from Chapter 3 will play out in the following chapters. The framework involves key stages and drivers that guide schools and districts through implementing new initiatives. This chapter outlines the stages of implementation and the core drivers that support successful implementation, providing examples of how schools and districts apply these principles in real-world settings.

Stages of Implementation

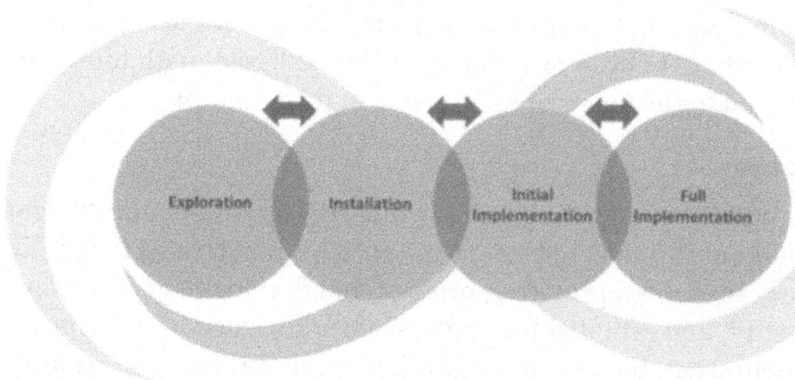

Figure 15.1. Stages of Implementation

Fixsen, D. L., & Blase, K. A. (2020). Active implementation frameworks. In P. Nilsen & S. A. Birken (Eds.), *Handbook on implementation science* (pp. 62–68). Edward Elgar Publishing.

Exploration

The exploration stage is the first phase of the implementation process. It involves identifying a school or district's needs, exploring potential evidence-based interventions, and assessing whether these interventions fit the local context well. During this stage, educators and administrators examine existing data, consult with stakeholders, and evaluate the feasibility of different approaches.

"The exploration stage sets the foundation for a successful implementation by identifying key needs and suitable interventions" (Bertram et al., 2015, p. 478). For example, in a suburban district facing declining literacy rates among early elementary students, the exploration stage might involve analyzing student performance data, reviewing various literacy interventions, and holding focus groups with teachers and parents to identify the most pressing needs. This stage ensures that the selected intervention aligns with the district's specific challenges and opportunities.

A real-world example of successful exploration can be seen in Jefferson County Public Schools in Kentucky. The district identified a need to improve math instruction in its elementary schools. Through the exploration phase, the district convened committees of teachers, administrators, and parents to review various math curricula and research-based interventions. By the end of the exploration stage, the district chose to adopt an evidence-based math intervention tailored to the needs of its students and community.

Installation

The installation stage focuses on preparing the school or district to implement the selected intervention. This involves securing the necessary resources, providing professional development and training for staff, and establishing the infrastructure needed to support implementation. Installation is crucial because it lays the groundwork for successful implementation.

"Installation is about laying the groundwork, ensuring that all necessary components are in place for effective implementation" (Fixsen et al., 2005, p. 480). For instance, in a rural district implementing a new science curriculum, the installation stage might involve purchasing the necessary materials, ensuring that teachers receive adequate training on the new instructional methods, and establishing a system for collecting and analyzing student assessment data.

An example of effective installation can be found in the San Diego Unified School District, which decided to implement a social-emotional learning (SEL) program across all K-12 schools. During the installation stage, the district invested in teacher training, developed a digital platform to track student progress, and established partnerships with community organizations to support the SEL program. By securing the necessary resources and support upfront, the district created the conditions for successful implementation.

Initial Implementation

The initial implementation stage is where the intervention is introduced into practice. Schools and districts often encounter challenges during this phase as they begin using the new intervention. Continuous monitoring, feedback loops, and real-time problem-solving are critical during this stage to address any issues that arise.

"Initial implementation often faces hurdles, requiring real-time problem-solving and adjustments" (Aarons et al., 2011, p. 8). For example, a school district implementing a new behavior management program may encounter resistance from teachers accustomed to their previous practices. To address this, the district might provide additional coaching and create opportunities for staff to share their concerns and experiences, adjusting the implementation as needed.

An illustrative case of initial implementation occurred in the Denver Public Schools system when the district introduced a new reading intervention for struggling readers. During the first few months, teachers reported difficulties integrating the intervention into their schedules. The district responded by providing additional coaching, revising the intervention's pacing guide, and offering teachers more flexibility in implementing the program. These adjustments helped smooth the initial implementation and ensured that the intervention was better aligned with the needs of the educators.

Full Implementation

Full implementation is achieved when the new practices are fully integrated into the school or district's daily routines. At this stage, the intervention is no longer seen as a new initiative but as the standard way of doing things. Consistency and ongoing monitoring are key components of full implementation.

"Full implementation is achieved when the new practices are fully embedded and consistently applied" (Fixsen et al., 2005, p. 15). For example, a district that has implemented a new data-driven instructional approach might reach full implementation when teachers routinely use data to inform their lesson planning, students are regularly assessed using the new methods, and administrators consistently support using data to drive decision-making.

Implementation Drivers

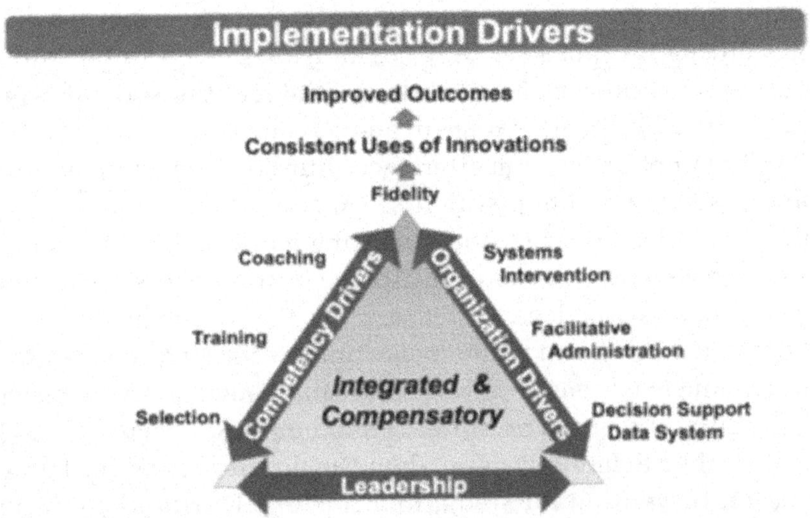

Figure 15.2. Implementation Drivers

Fixsen, D. L., & Blase, K. A. (2020). Active implementation frameworks. In P. Nilsen & S. A. Birken (Eds.), *Handbook on implementation science* (pp. 62–68). Edward Elgar Publishing.

Competency Drivers

Competency drivers are the mechanisms that ensure practitioners have the necessary skills and abilities to implement the intervention effectively. These drivers include professional development, ongoing coaching, and regular performance assessments. Competency drivers are essential because even the best interventions will fail if the individuals responsible for implementing them lack the necessary skills.

"Competency drivers focus on building and sustaining practitioner skills and abilities" (Fixsen et al., 2005, p. 29). For example, a district that introduces a new literacy program for early elementary students might provide ongoing coaching for teachers to help them master the instructional strategies required by the program. In addition, regular performance assessments may be used to identify areas where teachers need further support or training.

An example of competency drivers in action can be seen in Chicago Public Schools, where the district implemented a new approach to teaching mathematics. To build teacher capacity, the district provided a series of workshops and ongoing coaching throughout the year. Coaches observed teachers in their classrooms, offered feedback, and conducted small-group trainings to help teachers refine their practices. These competency drivers played a critical role in ensuring the successful implementation of the new math curriculum.

Organization Drivers

Organization drivers involve creating the supportive conditions within a school or district that facilitate successful implementation. These drivers include leadership support, data systems, and infrastructure that enable staff to implement the intervention effectively and sustainably. Organization drivers are essential for creating a school or district environment that is conducive to change.

"Organizational drivers are essential for creating the conditions that support and sustain implementation efforts" (Damschroder et al., 2009). For instance, a district implementing a new technology initiative may need to upgrade its technology infrastructure, provide ongoing technical support, and ensure that data systems are in place to monitor progress and outcomes.

In New York City's Department of Education, the district's efforts to integrate blended learning approaches required significant organizational drivers. The district upgraded its digital infrastructure, provided extensive IT support for schools, and established data systems to track student progress across digital platforms. By ensuring that the necessary organizational drivers were in place, New York City schools were able to effectively implement and sustain blended learning across a wide range of schools.

Leadership Drivers

Leadership drivers focus on the role of leadership in guiding the implementation process, maintaining focus on goals, and addressing challenges that arise. Effective leadership is critical to the success of any implementation effort. Leaders at both the school and district levels play a key role in ensuring that implementation efforts stay on track and that any issues are addressed in a timely manner.

"Leadership drivers ensure that there is clear direction, support, and accountability throughout the implementation process" (Aarons et al., 2011, p. 11). For example, in a district adopting a new disciplinary approach focused on restorative justice, strong leadership is essential to ensure that the new approach is embraced by staff and consistently applied across all schools. Leaders must also model the new practices and communicate clearly about expectations and progress.

An example of strong leadership drivers can be found in Montgomery County Public Schools in Maryland, where the district adopted a comprehensive equity initiative. District leaders provided clear direction, communicated the importance of the initiative to all stakeholders, and established accountability measures to track progress. School leaders were also empowered to guide the implementation at the building level, ensuring that the initiative was carried out with fidelity across the district.

Conclusion

The framework of Implementation Science provides schools and districts with a structured approach to integrating evidence-based practices into their daily operations. By following the stages of implementation—exploration, installation, initial implementation, and full implementation—schools can systematically adopt new initiatives that are tailored to their specific contexts. Additionally, the implementation drivers—competency, organization, and leadership —ensure that the necessary skills, supports, and leadership are in place to sustain these efforts over time.

Through careful planning, monitoring, and adjustment, schools and districts can successfully implement evidence-based interventions that lead to meaningful improvements in student outcomes. The Implementation Science framework offers a road map for navigating the complexities of educational change, ensuring that new practices are not only adopted but also maintained and integrated into the school or district's fabric.

Questions for Reflection

To deepen your understanding of the framework of Implementation Science and its application in education, consider the following questions:

1. What are the three "buckets" of Implementation Science, and what is the key point of the intended outcomes formula?
2. How does the exploration stage help ensure that schools and districts select the most appropriate interventions for their context?
3. What are some of the key actions taken during the installation stage, and why are they important for successful implementation?
4. How can schools address challenges that arise during the initial implementation stage?
5. What role do competency drivers play in ensuring that educators are prepared to implement new interventions effectively?
6. How can organizational and leadership drivers support the long-term sustainability of new practices in schools and districts?

Bibliography

Aarons, G. A., Hurlburt, M., & Horwitz, S. M. (2011). Advancing a conceptual model of evidence-based practice implementation in public service sectors. *Administration and Policy in Mental Health and Mental Health Services Research, 38*(1), 4–23.

Bertram, R. M., Blase, K. A., & Fixsen, D. L. (2015). Improving programs and outcomes: Implementation frameworks and organizational change. *Research on Social Work Practice, 25*(4), 477–487.

Damschroder, L. J., Aron, D. C., Keith, R. E., Kirsh, S. R., Alexander, J. A., & Lowery, J. C. (2009). Fostering implementation of health services research findings into practice: A consolidated framework for advancing implementation science. *Implementation Science, 4*(1), 50.

Fixsen, D. L., & Blase, K. A. (2020). Active implementation frameworks. In P. Nilsen & S. A. Birken (Eds.), *Handbook on implementation science* (pp. 62–68). Edward Elgar Publishing.

Fixsen, D. L., Blase, K. A., Naoom, S. F., & Wallace, F. (2005). Core implementation components. *Research on Social Work Practice, 15*(5), 531–539.

CHAPTER SIXTEEN

Implementing Evidence-Based Practices

School districts must establish robust systems to monitor progress and adapt strategies based on data-driven insights for educational initiatives to succeed. Monitoring systems allow districts to assess the effectiveness of their programs, identify areas for improvement, and ensure that resources are used efficiently to maximize student outcomes. This chapter explores the importance of continuous educational monitoring and adaptation, guiding how districts can build effective systems to track progress and make informed adjustments.

The Importance of Monitoring and Adaptation

Continuous Improvement

Continuous improvement is at the heart of effective educational management. By regularly monitoring progress, districts can make informed decisions about program adjustments, resource allocations, and instructional strategies. This ongoing process helps ensure that interventions remain relevant and effective in meeting students' needs.

"Continuous monitoring provides the feedback necessary for educational leaders to make data-driven decisions that enhance student learning and system efficiency" (Mandinach & Gummer, 2016). Data collected and analyzed consistently can illuminate areas where progress is being made and areas where strategies may need to be modified. For example, if a literacy intervention shows positive trends in some schools but lags in others, targeted adjustments can be made to address specific barriers in the underperforming schools.

Accountability

Robust monitoring systems also play a crucial role in increasing accountability within the education system. By measuring performance against predefined goals and standards, districts can ensure that educators and administrators are held accountable for providing a quality education to all students. These systems also help to demonstrate transparency and responsiveness to stakeholders, including parents, school boards, and the broader community.

"Accountability in education helps ensure that all students receive a quality education and that educators and administrators are responsive to student needs" (Darling-Hammond, 2010). Accountability fosters a sense of responsibility among educators and helps create a culture where continuous improvement is prioritized.

Building Effective Monitoring Systems

Establishing Clear Metrics and Goals

The foundation of an effective monitoring system begins with the establishment of clear, measurable goals and aligned metrics.

- **Goal Alignment:** Goals must be clearly defined and aligned with the district's broader objectives, such as improving literacy rates, closing achievement gaps, or increasing graduation rates. SMART goals—Specific, Measurable, Achievable, Relevant, and Time-bound—are a proven framework for guiding monitoring efforts. "Goals should be SMART to guide monitoring efforts effectively" (Doran, 1981, p. 35). For example, a district aiming to improve student math performance may set a SMART goal, such as increasing the percentage of students performing at grade level by 10% within 2 academic years.
- **Selection of Metrics:** Once goals are established, districts must select metrics that accurately reflect the critical aspects of the programs and implemented strategies. These metrics can include student achievement data, graduation rates, attendance records, disciplinary incidents, and other indicators of educational quality. The selected metrics should provide a comprehensive view of progress and be sensitive enough to detect changes over time.

Data Collection and Management

To monitor progress effectively, districts need to implement comprehensive data collection and management systems.

- **Comprehensive Data Collection:** A robust monitoring system collects diverse data types, including quantitative assessments (such as test scores) and qualitative feedback (such as surveys or focus group responses). "Effective data collection is comprehensive, capturing a range of indicators from academic performance to student and community feedback" (Bernhardt, 2013). For example, collecting both academic performance data and feedback from teachers and students about their experiences with a new instructional program can provide a fuller picture of its impact.
- **Data Management Systems:** Efficient data management systems are crucial for organizing, storing, and analyzing data in real time. Advanced data systems enable districts to conduct sophisticated analyses, identify trends, and make timely, data-driven decisions. "Advanced data systems enable more sophisticated analysis and more responsive educational practices" (Wayman, 2005, p. 3). By investing in high-quality data management tools, districts can ensure that data are accessible to educators and administrators, facilitating more informed and strategic decision-making.

Strategies for Data-Informed Adaptation

Data Analysis and Reporting

Regular analysis of collected data is essential for assessing progress and informing necessary adjustments to educational strategies.

- **Regular Data Analysis:** Conducting regular data analysis allows districts to track progress against established goals and benchmarks. This analysis should include examining trend data, identifying areas of success and underperformance, and comparing results with prior years or across schools. "Ongoing analysis helps identify trends that inform strategic adjustments and resource allocation" (Ikemoto & Marsh, 2007, p. 105). For instance, a district tracking student attendance data may identify patterns of chronic absenteeism among specific student groups, leading to targeted interventions.

- **Accessible Reporting:** Clear and accessible reports are necessary for communicating data insights to stakeholders, including school boards, teachers, parents, and students. Transparent reporting fosters trust and engagement from the broader community and enhances the accountability of educational systems. "Transparency in data reporting fosters trust and engagement from the community and enhances the accountability of educational systems" (Wayman & Cho, 2008).

Engaging Stakeholders in the Review Process

Stakeholder engagement is a vital component of the data-informed adaptation process. By involving a broad range of stakeholders, districts can enrich the review process and ensure that their strategies are responsive to the needs of the community.

- **Stakeholder Engagement:** Engaging teachers, students, parents, and community members in reviewing progress and planning adaptations provides valuable context and ensures that the district's strategies are inclusive and equitable. "Engagement with a broad range of stakeholders enriches the review process and supports more effective adaptations" (Bryk et al., 2010). For example, hosting community forums to discuss progress on district initiatives can lead to more informed and contextually relevant decisions.
- **Feedback Mechanisms:** Implementing formal feedback mechanisms allows districts to collect ongoing input from stakeholders throughout the school year. This feedback can be collected through surveys, focus groups, or online platforms that allow stakeholders to voice their experiences and perspectives. "Feedback is a powerful tool for improvement, providing a direct line to stakeholder experiences and perceptions" (Hattie, 2009, p. 12). Incorporating this feedback into decision-making ensures that the district remains responsive to the needs of students and the community.

Adapting Strategies Based on Monitoring

Iterative Process

Effective adaptation is an iterative process that involves continuous cycles of planning, action, and reflection.

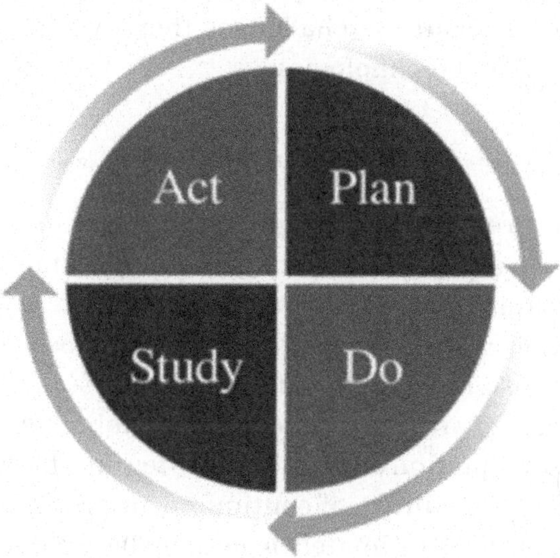

Figure 16.1. PDSA Cycle

Fixsen, D. L., & Blase, K. A. (2020). Active implementation frameworks. In P. Nilsen & S. A. Birken (Eds.), *Handbook on implementation science* (pp. 62–68). Edward Elgar Publishing.

- **Plan-Do-Study-Act (PDSA) Cycles:** One widely used model for continuous improvement is the Plan-Do-Study-Act (PDSA) cycle. This process involves planning a change, implementing the change, studying the results, and acting on what is learned. "The PDSA cycle is a classic tool for continuous improvement in educational settings and beyond" (Deming, 1986). In an educational context, districts may use PDSA cycles to implement new instructional strategies, monitor their impact on student achievement, and adjust the approach as needed.
- **Responsive Adjustments:** Making timely adjustments to strategies based on data insights is crucial for ensuring that educational programs remain effective and aligned with student

needs. Adaptations may involve reallocating resources, modifying instructional approaches, or providing additional supports to struggling students. "Adaptation is key to ensuring that educational strategies remain effective and responsive to student needs" (Fullan, 2007, p. 84). For example, a district might adjust its professional development offerings based on feedback from teachers about the challenges they face in implementing new instructional technologies.

Conclusion

Monitoring progress and adapting strategies are essential components of effective educational management. By establishing robust monitoring systems, districts can ensure that their programs are aligned with their goals, responsive to student needs, and grounded in data-driven insights. Effective monitoring systems require clear metrics, comprehensive data collection, stakeholder engagement, and responsive adaptation strategies. By integrating these elements, districts can foster a culture of continuous improvement, accountability, and innovation, ultimately leading to better educational outcomes for all students.

Questions for Reflection

To deepen your understanding of how to build effective monitoring systems and adapt strategies based on data insights, consider the following questions:

1. How can districts establish measurable goals aligning with their broader objectives and effectively guide monitoring efforts?
2. Why is it important to use a combination of quantitative and qualitative data when assessing the effectiveness of educational programs?
3. What role does stakeholder engagement play in the monitoring and adaptation process, and how can districts ensure they effectively involve all relevant stakeholders?

4. How can districts use the Plan-Do-Study-Act (PDSA) cycle to improve their educational strategies continuously, and what are the benefits of this iterative approach?
5. What challenges might districts face in adapting strategies based on monitoring data, and how can they address them to ensure their interventions remain effective?

Bibliography

Bernhardt, V. L. (2013). *Data analysis for continuous school improvement.* Routledge.

Bryk, A. S., Sebring, P. B., Allensworth, E., Luppescu, S., & Easton, J. Q. (2010). *Organizing schools for improvement: Lessons from Chicago.* University of Chicago Press.

Darling-Hammond, L. (2010). *The flat world and education: How America's commitment to equity will determine our future.* Teachers College Press.

Deming, W. E. (1986). *Out of the crisis.* MIT Press.

Doran, G. T. (1981). There's a S.M.A.R.T. way to write management's goals and objectives. *Management Review, 70*(11), 35–36.

Fullan, M. (2007). *The new meaning of educational change.* Teachers College Press.

Hattie, J. (2009). *Visible learning: A synthesis of over 800 meta-analyses relating to achievement.* Routledge.

Ikemoto, G. S., & Marsh, J. A. (2007). Cutting through the "data-driven" mantra: Different conceptions of data-driven decision making. *Yearbook of the National Society for the Study of Education, 106*(1), 105–131.

Mandinach, E. B., & Gummer, E. S. (2016). *Data literacy for educators: Making it count in teacher preparation and practice.* Teachers College Press.

Wayman, J. C. (2005). Involving teachers in data-driven decision making: Using computer data systems to support teacher inquiry and reflection. *Journal of Education for Students Placed at Risk, 10*(3), 295–308.

Wayman, J. C., & Cho, V. (2008). Preparing educators to effectively use student data systems. In T. J. Kowalski & T. J. Lasley (Eds.), *Handbook on data-based decision-making in education* (pp. 89–104). Routledge.

CHAPTER SEVENTEEN

Case Studies

The success of educational initiatives hinges on a school district's ability to monitor progress effectively and make data-driven adaptations to their strategies. Case studies of districts that successfully implement robust monitoring systems offer valuable lessons for other educational leaders. This chapter explores two case studies that illustrate how districts have used innovative approaches to monitor progress, engage stakeholders, and make timely adjustments to improve student outcomes. These examples demonstrate the power of data dashboards and community-engaged review processes in driving meaningful improvements in education.

Case Studies and Examples

Example 1: Inclusive Curriculum Review in an Urban District

An urban school district in California recognized the need to update its curriculum to reflect the cultural diversity of its student population. The district implemented an inclusive curriculum review process involving teachers, administrators, students, and community members to address this. The inclusive approach allowed the district to hear from stakeholders often underrepresented in decision-making processes.

As a result, the district adopted a more culturally responsive curriculum that better met the needs of its diverse student body. The inclusion of student and community voices led to the incorporation of local histories, culturally relevant literature, and instructional materials that represented the students' experiences.

"Our inclusive process ensured that all voices were heard and that our curriculum reflected the diversity of our community" (García-Carmona & Oplatka, 2024). This case demonstrates how engaging a broad range of stakeholders through Implementation Science principles can lead to more relevant and inclusive educational practices that resonate with the local community.

Example 2: A District Using Data Dashboards

In a suburban school district in the Midwest, district leaders recognized the need for a more efficient and effective way to monitor student performance and engagement. The district implemented a data dashboard that provides real-time access to critical metrics, such as attendance, grades, and behavioral data, allowing administrators and teachers to identify issues and intervene promptly.

The data dashboard aggregates information from various sources, including student information systems, learning management platforms, and attendance records. By integrating these data streams, the dashboard provides a comprehensive view of each student's academic progress and engagement. Teachers and administrators can easily access this information and receive alerts when a student's performance or attendance declines.

For example, suppose a student's attendance starts to drop. In that case, the system automatically flags the issue, allowing school staff to quickly reach out to the student and their family to offer support. Similarly, if a student's grades start to decline, teachers can intervene by offering additional help, adjusting instructional strategies, or providing targeted tutoring.

"Data dashboards provide immediate insights crucial for timely interventions" (Johnson, 2021). The dashboard has also enabled the district to monitor progress toward its broader goals, such as improving graduation rates and closing achievement gaps. By regularly reviewing dashboard data at the district and school levels, administrators can identify trends, allocate resources more effectively, and ensure that all students receive the support they need.

Impact of Data Dashboards

Since implementing the dashboard, the district has reported significant improvements in student outcomes. Attendance rates have increased due to timely interventions, and student performance has improved, particularly among students previously at risk of falling behind. The dashboard has also helped streamline communication between teachers, administrators, and parents, fostering a more collaborative approach to student support.

Example 2: Community-Engaged Review Process in an Urban District

In an urban school district on the East Coast, district leaders sought to improve the relevance and effectiveness of their educational programs by involving the community more deeply in the evaluation and review process. The district established a community-engaged review process that invites parents, local organizations, and other community stakeholders to evaluate the district's programs and initiatives.

Community Engagement in Monitoring

The community-engaged review process involves regular meetings between district leaders, parents, and representatives from local organizations such as nonprofits, businesses, and advocacy groups. During these meetings, participants review data on student performance, program effectiveness, and resource allocation and discuss how the district's programs align with community needs and priorities.

This collaborative approach allows community members to provide feedback on existing programs and offer suggestions for new initiatives that better serve the district's diverse population. For instance, parents in one community expressed concern about the lack of after-school programs for middle school students. In response, the district partnered with a local nonprofit to develop an after-school enrichment program that provides academic support, recreation, and career exploration opportunities for middle schoolers.

"Engaging the community in the monitoring process helps ensure that educational programs are relevant and effectively supported" (U.S. Agency for International Development, n.d.). By involving community stakeholders in the review process, the district has been able to tailor its programs better to meet the needs of its students and families while also increasing public support for its initiatives.

Impact of Community Engagement

The community-engaged review process has led to several positive outcomes for the district. Educational programs are now more closely aligned with the community's needs and values, resulting in increased participation in programs such as after-school activities and family literacy nights. Additionally, the process has strengthened relationships between the district and community organizations, leading to new partnerships and increased student resources.

Public support for district initiatives has also grown as community members feel more invested in the success of the district's programs. This support has translated into stronger advocacy for the district's funding needs and greater collaboration between schools and local organizations.

Lessons Learned From Case Studies

The case studies highlighted in this chapter demonstrate key lessons about the role of inclusive decision-making, data-driven monitoring, and community engagement in successfully implementing educational initiatives. First, stakeholder inclusion is vital for developing curricula and programs that reflect the diverse needs of students and the broader community. In the case of the California district, involving students, teachers, and community members in the curriculum review process ensured that the resulting materials were culturally responsive and relevant. This inclusive approach led to more meaningful learning experiences and fostered a sense of ownership and buy-in from all parties involved. This example emphasizes that diverse perspectives in curriculum development lead to better educational outcomes by addressing students' specific needs and backgrounds (García-Carmona & Oplatka, 2024).

Second, real-time data systems such as dashboards provide districts with critical tools to monitor student progress and intervene early when problems arise. The Midwest district's implementation of a data dashboard allowed teachers and administrators to identify attendance or academic issues before they escalated. By giving educators timely, actionable data, the district could target support to students who needed it most, leading to improved student performance and attendance (Johnson, 2021). This example underscores the importance of having efficient data systems that allow for immediate, informed decision-making, ultimately benefiting students at risk of falling behind.

Third, community engagement in monitoring and reviewing programs can ensure that educational initiatives remain relevant to the needs of the local population. The East Coast district's approach involved parents, nonprofits, and local businesses in reviewing and shaping programs, leading to developing initiatives that better aligned with the community's values and needs, such as after-school programs for middle schoolers. This collaborative model resulted in more tailored educational solutions and increased community support for the district's efforts, leading to stronger partnerships and greater advocacy for funding and resources (U.S. Agency for International Development, n.d.). This lesson illustrates how engaging external stakeholders in program review can enrich educational offerings and foster long-term community investment in schools.

Finally, both case studies highlight the importance of sustained leadership and accountability. District leaders who actively supported the integration of inclusive curriculum reviews, data dashboards, and community-engaged processes ensured these initiatives were prioritized and sustained over time. Leadership was essential in maintaining the momentum for continuous improvement, allocating necessary resources, and creating an environment that welcomed feedback and collaboration. Strong leadership ensures that innovative practices are implemented, monitored, and adapted to changing conditions.

Questions for Reflection

To deepen your understanding of how to build effective monitoring systems and adapt strategies based on data insights, consider the following questions:

1. How can your district or school involve a more diverse group of stakeholders—teachers, students, parents, and community

members—in the curriculum review and program monitoring process? What structures or systems can be established to ensure ongoing, meaningful input from these groups?

2. Does your school or district have access to real-time data systems, such as dashboards, that allow for timely identification of student needs? How can these systems be used more effectively to inform instructional practices, monitor progress, and support struggling students?
3. How can your district strengthen its collaboration with community organizations, local businesses, and families to ensure educational programs align with community priorities? How can you create regular feedback and partnership development opportunities with these external stakeholders?
4. How can district and school leaders ensure that new initiatives, such as data monitoring systems or community engagement processes, are sustained over time? What mechanisms can be put in place to hold leaders and educators accountable for maintaining their integrity and effectiveness?
5. How can your school or district balance fidelity to evidence-based practices with the flexibility to adapt programs to local contexts? What processes can be established to evaluate whether adaptations are necessary and to ensure they do not compromise the effectiveness of the intervention?

Bibliography

U.S. Agency for International Development. (n.d.). *Community engagement in education: Guidelines and best practices.* https://www.edu-links.org

García-Carmona, M., & Oplatka, I. (2024). Leading intercultural schools: The role of attentiveness in cultural diverse contexts. *International Journal of Leadership in Education, 27*(3), 705–714.

Johnson, S. (2021). Optimizing school operations through data insights. *Journal of School Leadership, 31*(2), 123–145.

CONCLUSION

As we conclude *Implementation Science: A Playbook for Instructional Leaders*, we reflect on the journey of translating evidence-based practices into actionable strategies that can transform your educational setting and outcomes. This journey, which began with understanding the research-to-practice gap and the pressing need for evidence-based practices, has emphasized the importance of a structured approach to educational reform. Implementation Science is more than a methodology; it is a guiding framework that enables instructional leaders to convert research into practical, impactful change that endures in real-world educational settings.

This final chapter synthesizes the key ideas covered in this book, from selecting high-quality instructional materials to building cohesive teams, establishing usable innovations, and evaluating progress. As instructional leaders look ahead, this chapter also offers insights into the path forward, reinforcing the roles of reflection, adaptability, and community in driving sustained improvements. By building on the principles and strategies detailed in this playbook, instructional leaders are well-equipped to guide their schools and districts toward meaningful, lasting transformation.

Key Themes and Insights

1. The Importance of Usable Innovation

Effective implementation begins with a strong foundation: a clearly defined and usable innovation. Whether it's a curriculum, an instructional strategy, or a student support system, ensuring that the innovation is well-documented, aligned with core values, and scalable is critical. Usable innovations are those that can be applied consistently across diverse educational settings without losing effectiveness. Leaders should prioritize selecting or developing programs that have clear essential functions, operational definitions, and performance assessments that allow for ongoing evaluation. By doing so, they establish a program that is not only effective in theory but can also be adapted to meet the unique needs of their schools and students in practice.

2. Building and Supporting Effective Teams

No implementation effort succeeds without the collaborative efforts of a well-organized team. The process of building curriculum review and implementation teams, discussed in depth in this book, highlighted the importance of assembling diverse groups that bring varied perspectives and expertise. Teams should include representation from all levels of the educational community—administrators, teachers, specialists, parents, and even students where appropriate. Such inclusivity fosters shared ownership, which is essential for buy-in and sustained commitment. Leaders must continue to prioritize shared leadership, creating a structure where team members feel valued and empowered to contribute meaningfully to the implementation process.

3. The Role of Strategic Planning in Implementation

Strategic planning is the road map that guides successful implementation, ensuring that each phase is well-defined, resourced, and monitored. Leaders have learned that without a clear vision, timeline, and strategic framework, even the best innovations may falter in the complex realities of educational settings. Planning involves not only setting goals but also determining how progress will be measured, how resources will be allocated, and how feedback will be collected to make timely adjustments. Instructional leaders are encouraged to keep strategic planning at the forefront, continually revisiting and adjusting plans as the program unfolds to maintain alignment with goals and respond to emerging needs.

4. Data-Driven Decision-Making and Continuous Improvement

Throughout the book, we emphasized the power of data in guiding implementation decisions and sustaining improvements. Instructional leaders must gather, analyze, and act on data consistently to inform every stage of the implementation journey—from needs assessment and baseline setting to monitoring progress and assessing outcomes. This commitment to data-driven decision-making fosters a culture of continuous improvement, allowing leaders and educators to refine practices, address challenges proactively, and celebrate successes along the way. Leaders should prioritize accessible and meaningful data collection tools that empower educators to understand their impact and make informed adjustments that benefit students.

5. Sustaining Innovations through Adaptability and Resilience

The ultimate goal of Implementation Science is to ensure that effective practices become embedded in the culture and operations of educational settings, leading to sustained change. However, sustaining innovations requires flexibility and adaptability. Instructional leaders must be prepared to support their teams through shifts in policy, funding, staffing, or student needs, ensuring that essential components of innovations remain intact while adapting to evolving circumstances. Cultivating resilience within teams and building a supportive infrastructure can help schools and districts overcome obstacles and continue to deliver impactful educational experiences for students.

Path Forward for Instructional Leaders

The path forward for instructional leaders is one of commitment to learning, adaptation, and continual growth. Implementation Science does not offer a single solution but instead provides a framework that evolves with experience and insight. As instructional leaders apply the principles from this playbook in their own schools and districts, they will likely encounter unexpected challenges. Embracing these challenges as opportunities for learning and improvement is fundamental to sustaining change and achieving lasting success.

Instructional leaders are also encouraged to foster a community of practice within their districts and beyond. By sharing experiences, challenges, and successes with other leaders, they contribute to a broader understanding of what works in education. This collaborative approach not only strengthens individual implementation efforts but also advances the field of Implementation Science as a whole.

As instructional leaders reflect on their work, a few guiding questions can help deepen their understanding and enhance their impact:

- What are the core values and goals driving our implementation efforts, and how well do they align with the needs of our students and community?
- How can we ensure that our team remains motivated, collaborative, and committed to the innovation as it becomes embedded in our educational practices?
- What data do we need to effectively monitor progress, and how can we make data collection and analysis a meaningful and empowering process for all stakeholders?
- How can we create a culture of adaptability that supports the innovation's resilience in the face of challenges and changes?
- What steps can we take to share our learning, successes, and challenges with the broader educational community to contribute to the collective knowledge of Implementation Science in education?

Conclusion

The journey of implementing evidence-based practices through the lens of Implementation Science is one of thoughtful planning, collaborative effort, and reflective growth. As instructional leaders work to bridge the research-to-practice gap, they become agents of change dedicated to making a positive difference in the lives of students and communities. This playbook serves as a resource and guide, but it is the commitment of leaders and educators to continually learn, adapt, and innovate that will ultimately drive sustainable improvement.

By following the principles and strategies outlined in *Implementation Science: A Playbook for Instructional Leaders*, educational leaders are equipped not only to make immediate impacts but also to lay the foundation for enduring change. This journey is one of commitment, resilience, and the shared goal of fostering educational environments where every student has the opportunity to succeed.

BIBLIOGRAPHY

Aarons, G. A., Hurlburt, M., & Horwitz, S. M. (2011). Advancing a conceptual model of evidence-based practice implementation in public service sectors. *Administration and Policy in Mental Health and Mental Health Services Research, 38*(1), 4–23.

Arkansas Department of Education. (2019). *Right to Read Act.* https://dese.ade.arkansas.gov

Bernhardt, V. L. (2013). *Data analysis for continuous school improvement.* Routledge.

Bertram, R. M., Blase, K. A., & Fixsen, D. L. (2015). Improving programs and outcomes: Implementation frameworks and organizational change. *Research on Social Work Practice, 25*(4), 477–487.

Best Evidence Encyclopedia. (n.d.). http://www.bestevidence.org/

Bryk, A. S., Gomez, L. M., Grunow, A., & LeMahieu, P. G. (2015). *Learning to improve: How America's schools can get better at getting better.* Harvard Education Press.

Bryk, A. S., Sebring, P. B., Allensworth, E., Luppescu, S., & Easton, J. Q. (2010). *Organizing schools for improvement: Lessons from Chicago.* University of Chicago Press.

Bryson, J. M. (2018). *Strategic planning for public and nonprofit organizations: A guide to strengthening and sustaining organizational achievement.* John Wiley & Sons.

Century, J., & Cassata, A. (2016). Conceptual foundations for measuring the implementation of educational innovations. *Journal of Educational Research, 109*(1), 1–19.

Choi, H., & Drago-Severson, E. (2023). Helping teacher leadership teams: Enhancing teaming by focusing knowledge integration. *European Journal of Educational Management, 6*(2), 69-82. https://doi.org/10.12973/eujem.6.2.69

Damschroder, L. J., Aron, D. C., Keith, R. E., Kirsh, S. R., Alexander, J. A., & Lowery, J. C. (2009). Fostering implementation of health services research findings into practice: A consolidated framework for advancing implementation science. *Implementation Science, 4*(1), 50.

Darling-Hammond, L. (2010). *The flat world and education: How America's commitment to equity will determine our future.* Teachers College Press.

Darling-Hammond, L., LaPointe, M., Meyerson, D., Orr, M. T., & Cohen, C. (2010). *Preparing principals for a changing world: Lessons from effective school leadership programs.* Jossey-Bass.

Deming, W. E. (1986). *Out of the crisis.* MIT Press.

Desimone, L. M., & Garet, M. S. (2015). Best practices in teachers' professional development in the United States. *Psychology, Society & Education, 7*(3), 252–263.

Doran, G. T. (1981). There's a S.M.A.R.T. way to write management's goals and objectives. *Management Review, 70*(11), 35–36.

DuFour, R., & Eaker, R. (1998). *Professional learning communities at work: Best practices for enhancing student achievement.* Solution Tree.

DuFour, R., & Marzano, R. J. (2011). *Leaders of learning: How district, school, and classroom leaders improve student achievement.* Solution Tree.

Durlak, J. A., & DuPre, E. P. (2008). Implementation matters: A review of research on the influence of implementation on program outcomes and the factors affecting implementation. *American Journal of Community Psychology, 41*(3), 327–350.

Dusenbury, L., Brannigan, R., Falco, M., & Hansen, W. B. (2003). A review of research on fidelity of implementation: Implications for drug abuse prevention in school settings. *Health Education Research, 18*(2), 237–256.

Fixsen, D. L., & Blase, K. A. (2020). Active implementation frameworks. In P. Nilsen & S. A. Birken (Eds.), *Handbook on implementation science* (pp. 62–68). Edward Elgar Publishing.

Fixsen, D., Blase, K., Metz, A., & Van Dyke, M. (2015). Implementation science. In R. Joshi & S. Paciorek (Eds.), *The future of evidence-based education* (pp. 14–25). Harvard Education Press.

Fixsen, D. L., Blase, K. A., Naoom, S. F., & Wallace, F. (2005). Core implementation components. *Research on Social Work Practice, 15*(5), 531–539.

Fixsen, D. L., Naoom, S. F., Blase, K. A., Friedman, R. M., & Wallace, F. (2013). *Implementation research: A synthesis of the literature.* University of South Florida, Louis de la Parte Florida Mental Health Institute, The National Implementation Research Network.

Freeman, R. E. (2015). *Strategic management: A stakeholder approach.* Cambridge University Press.

Fullan, M. (2007). *The new meaning of educational change.* Teachers College Press.

Fullan, M. (2011). *The moral imperative realized.* Corwin Press.

Garcia, M. (2022). Inclusive curriculum review: A case study in urban education. *Journal of Multicultural Education.*

Garmston, R. J., & Wellman, B. M. (2016). *The adaptive school: A sourcebook for developing collaborative groups.* Rowman & Littlefield.

Gay, G. (2018). *Culturally responsive teaching: Theory, research, and practice.* Teachers College Press.

Guskey, T. R. (2002). Professional development and teacher change. *Teachers and Teaching: Theory and Practice, 8*(3), 381–391.

Hanford, E. (2019). Hard words: Why aren't kids being taught to read? *APM Reports.*

Hanford, E. (Producer). (2022). *Sold a Story* [Podcast]. APM Reports, Minnesota Public Radio. https://www.apmreports.org

Hart, R. (1992). *Children's participation: From tokenism to citizenship.* UNICEF International Child Development Centre.

Hattie, J. (2009). *Visible learning: A synthesis of over 800 meta-analyses relating to achievement.* Routledge.

Heath, C., & Heath, D. (2010). *Switch: How to change things when change is hard.* Broadway Books.

Henderson, A. T., & Mapp, K. L. (2002). *A new wave of evidence: The impact of school, family, and community connections on student achievement.* National Center for Family & Community Connections with Schools.

Ikemoto, G. S., & Marsh, J. A. (2007). Cutting through the "data-driven" mantra: Different conceptions of data-driven decision making. *Yearbook of the National Society for the Study of Education, 106*(1), 105–131.

Johnson, S. (2021). Optimizing school operations through data insights. *Journal of School Leadership, 31*(2), 123–145

Jones, L. (2018). Effective practices for sharing innovation in schools. *Educational Leadership Journal.*

Joyce, B., & Showers, B. (2002). *Student achievement through staff development.* ASCD.

Kerr, K., Kavanaugh, L., & Rappaport, S. (2016). *The strategic data project toolkit for effective data use.* Harvard Education Press.

Kilpatrick, D. A. (2015). *Essentials of assessing, preventing, and overcoming reading difficulties.* Wiley.

Kotter, J. P. (1996). *Leading change.* Harvard Business Review Press.

Kouzes, J. M., & Posner, B. Z. (2012). *The leadership challenge: How to make extraordinary things happen in organizations.* Jossey-Bass.

Leithwood, K., Seashore Louis, K., Anderson, S., & Wahlstrom, K. (2004). *How leadership influences student learning.* Wallace Foundation.

Loewus, L. (2020, January 14). *How Mississippi's Approach to Reading Instruction is Paying Off.* Education Week. https://www.edweek.org

Mackenzie, J. (Director). (2023). *The Right to Read* [Film]. Tribeca Films.

Maddox, A., & Feng, L. (2021). *Leadership for literacy: The role of administrators in supporting effective reading instruction.* Journal of Educational Leadership, 45(3), 180–195.

Mandinach, E. B., & Gummer, E. S. (2016). *Data literacy for educators: Making it count in teacher preparation and practice.* Teachers College Press.

Marzano, R. J., Waters, T., & McNulty, B. A. (2005). *School leadership that works: From research to results.* ASCD.

Mississippi Department of Education. (2021). *Literacy-Based Promotion Act Update.* https://www.mdek12.org

Moats, L. C. (2020). *Teaching reading is rocket science: What expert teachers of reading should know and be able to do.* American Federation of Teachers.

Page, S. E. (2007). *The difference: How the power of diversity creates better groups, firms, schools, and societies.* Princeton University Press.

Pink, D. H. (2009). *Drive: The surprising truth about what motivates us.* Riverhead Books.

Putnam, R. D. (2000). *Bowling alone: The collapse and revival of American community.* Simon & Schuster.

Robinson, K. (2015). *Creative schools: The grassroots revolution that's transforming education.* Viking.

Sanders, M. G. (2018). *Schooling students placed at risk: Research, policy, and practice in the education of poor and minority adolescents.* Lawrence Erlbaum Associates.

Santoro, L. E. (2020). The critical role of leadership in literacy instruction: Supporting evidence-based practices. *Reading Research Quarterly, 55*(S1), S123–S136.

Senge, P. M. (2006). *The fifth discipline: The art and practice of the learning organization.* Doubleday.

Shanahan, T. (2020). What constitutes evidence-based literacy instruction? *Reading Research Quarterly, 55*(S1), S361-S372.

Sleeter, C. E. (2017). *Multicultural education as social activism.* SUNY Press.

Smith, A. (2020). Diverse perspectives in curriculum review: Ensuring equity and inclusion. *Journal of Curriculum Studies.*

Smith, A. (2021). Empowering teacher leaders: A case study in distributed leadership. *Journal of Educational Change, 6*(1), 122–127

Spillane, J. P. (2006). *Distributed leadership.* Jossey-Bass.

Thapa, A., Cohen, J., Guffey, S., & Higgins-D'Alessandro, A. (2013). A review of school climate research. *Review of Educational Research, 83*(3), 357–385.

Tucker, C. (2021). Rigor and relevance in curriculum development. *Educational Leadership Review, 22*(1), 75–90.

U.S. Department of Education. (2020). *Comprehensive literacy state development grants.* https://www.ed.gov

Wayman, J. C. (2005). Involving teachers in data-driven decision making: Using computer data systems to support teacher inquiry and reflection. *Journal of Education for Students Placed at Risk, 10*(3), 295–308.

What Works Clearinghouse. (n.d.). *Home.* Institute of Education Sciences. https://ies.ed.gov/ncee/wwc/

Zhao, Y. (2015). *Who's afraid of the big bad dragon: Why China has the best (and worst) education system in the world.* Jossey-Bass.

ABOUT THE AUTHOR

Dr. Julia James Carlson is an accomplished educational leader with over two decades of experience in school turnaround, curriculum development/management, and instructional leadership. With a career spanning urban, suburban, and rural districts, private sectors, and nonprofit organizations, Dr. Carlson has become a trusted voice in educational reform and Implementation Science. She holds an Ed.D. in educational administration from Boston College, where she received the prestigious AASA Educational Administrative Scholarship Award.

Dr. Carlson's career is marked by a deep commitment to improving student outcomes through evidence-based practices and collaborative leadership. She has served in various roles, including product management director: Implementation Science at Imagine Learning, vice president of Research at Wilson Language Training, Invention Education administrator at the Massachusetts Institute of Technology (MIT), and assistant superintendent of Fall River Public Schools. In these positions, she led initiatives to enhance literacy instruction, developed and implemented innovative educational programs, and district-wide data systems to monitor student progress. Her leadership was pivotal in securing multi-million-dollar grants and raising student achievement rates in underperforming school districts.

As a passionate advocate for literacy and equity in education, Dr. Carlson has presented nationally on the role of Implementation Science in school reform, focusing on creating supportive climates for administrator and teacher development and improving literacy outcomes. She was also a Collaborative Teaching Fellow and practicum supervisor at Boston College, mentoring future educators and preparing them to thrive in urban education settings through the Donovan Scholars Program. Dr. Carlson's extensive experience in K-12 and higher education underscores her holistic understanding of the educational landscape. In addition to her work stateside, she has been a mentor for the global organization, Worldwide SHEroes, explicitly working with aspiring female education leaders in Africa.

Dr. Carlson is an active member of professional organizations such as the American Educational Research Association and the International Dyslexia Association. She was a key stakeholder in developing the Massachusetts Dyslexia Guidelines, co-developed by the Departments of Elementary and Secondary Education and Early Education and Care, to implement specific requirements of An Act Relative to Students with Dyslexia, Chapter 272 of the Acts of 2018. In addition to her advocacy and lobbying for early access to education, she has co-authored several publications, including work on structured literacy and educational leadership. She has been invited to present at prestigious conferences nationwide.

Dr. Carlson lives in Providence, Rhode Island with her husband and two sons, who inspire her daily. Her work continues to be guided by a passion for ensuring that all students, regardless of background, have access to high-quality education and the tools they need to succeed.

INDEX